Breakthroughs

An Integrated Upper Intermediate English Program

Workbook

Gloria McPherson-Ramirez
Marina Engelking

OXFORD
UNIVERSITY PRESS

OXFORD
UNIVERSITY PRESS

Oxford University Press is a department of the University of Oxford.
It furthers the University's objective of excellence in research, scholarship, and education
by publishing worldwide. Oxford is a registered trade mark of Oxford University Press in the UK
and in certain other countries.

Published in Canada by
Oxford University Press
8 Sampson Mews, Suite 204,
Don Mills, Ontario M3C 0H5 Canada

www.oupcanada.comCopyright © Oxford University Press Canada 2012

The moral rights of the author have been asserted

Database right Oxford University Press (maker)

First Edition published in 2012

All rights reserved. No part of this publication may be reproduced, stored in a retrieval system, or transmitted, in any form or by any means, without the prior permission in writing of Oxford University Press, or as expressly permitted by law, by licence, or under terms agreed with the appropriate reprographics rights organization. Enquiries concerning reproduction outside the scope of the above should be sent to the Permissions Department at the address above or through the following url: www.oupcanada.com/permission/permission_request.php

Every effort has been made to determine and contact copyright holders. In the case of any omissions, the publisher will be pleased to make suitable acknowledgement in future editions.

Library and Archives Canada Cataloguing in Publication

McPherson-Ramirez, Gloria, 1963–
Breakthroughs : an integrated upper intermediate English program. Workbook /
Gloria McPherson-Ramirez, Marina Engelking.

ISBN 978-0-19-543226-8

1. English language—Problems, exercises, etc.
2. English language—Textbooks for second language
learners. I. Engelking, Marina, 1959– II. Title.

PE1112.M43 2010 Suppl. 1   428.2'4   C2009-907125-8

Cover image: © iStockphoto.com/John Kropewnicki

Printed and bound in Canada

2 3 4 — 18 17 16

Contents

UNIT 1 Hero to the Rescue!	1
Vocabulary	1
Vocabulary Expansion	1
Grammar Focus: Adverbs of Manner	2
Reading	3
Writing: Narrative Paragraphs	4
Academic Word List	7

UNIT 2 Ancient Secrets Revealed	9
Vocabulary	9
Grammar Focus: Past Time	10
Reading	12
Writing: Paragraphs That Compare and Contrast	12
Academic Word List	16

UNIT 3 O Canada, Je t'aime	19
Vocabulary	19
Grammar Focus: Quantifiers	20
Reading	21
Writing: Descriptive Paragraphs	22
Academic Word List	26

UNIT 4 Stay Tuned!	28
Vocabulary	28
Vocabulary Expansion	29
Grammar Focus: Reported Speech	30
Reading	33
Writing: Persuasive Paragraphs	33
Academic Word List	37

UNIT 5 Buyer Beware!	39
Vocabulary	39
Vocabulary Expansion	40
Grammar Focus: Gerunds	41
Reading	44
Writing: Expository Paragraphs	44
Academic Word List	47

UNIT 6 Catch Me If You Can	50
Vocabulary	50
Vocabulary Expansion	52
Grammar Focus: Passive Voice	52
Reading	54
Writing: Process Paragraphs	55
Academic Word List	58

UNIT 7 Doing the Right Thing	61
Vocabulary	61
Vocabulary Expansion	62
Grammar Focus: Unreal and Real Conditionals	63
Reading	65
Writing: Cause-and-Effect Paragraphs	65
Academic Word List	69

UNIT 8 Love Is in the Air	73
Vocabulary	73
Vocabulary Expansion	74
Grammar Focus: Adjective Clauses	74
Reading	77
Writing: Paragraphs That Compare and Contrast	77
Academic Word List	82

UNIT 9 Get Those Creative Juices Flowing!	85
Vocabulary	85
Grammar Focus: Information Questions	86
Reading	88
Writing: Narrative Paragraphs	89
Academic Word List	93

UNIT 10 That's So Canadian	95
Vocabulary	95
Grammar Focus: Articles	97
Reading	98
Writing: Definition Paragraphs	99
Academic Word List	103

Answer Key	106

Appendix	135

Unit 1
Hero to the Rescue!

Vocabulary

Exercise A

Replace the italicized words in the following sentences with more precise words from the following list:

dedicated	persistent	well-respected
honest	selfless	
innovative	trustworthy	

1. He is a very *thoughtful person who always thinks about the needs of others*. The world would be a better place if more people were like him!
2. She is a very *determined person who does things even when they are difficult*. She doesn't let anything stop her from accomplishing her goals.
3. He is known for being *truthful and never stealing or cheating*. You can always trust him.
4. She is *admired for her good qualities and achievements* by everyone who meets her or works with her.
5. He's *putting a lot of time and effort into his job*. His work is very important to him.
6. She is someone who is *extremely honest, good, and dependable*. You can always rely on her.
7. That is a *new and unique* product.

Exercise B

Complete the crossword by filling in the blanks using words from the box.

amazing	extraordinary	rescue
courage	injustice	sacrifice
criminals	powers	

Across

4. Astonishing and wonderful
6. People involved in breaking the law
7. Greater than expected, surprising or strange
8. Specific abilities of the mind or body

Down

1. Give up something important in order to do something that seems more important
2. An unfair situation where people are not treated equally
3. To save someone from a harmful situation
5. The ability to face danger or fear

Vocabulary Expansion

Exercise C

Villains (evil characters) have negative characteristics that often contrast with the positive characteristics of heroes. Complete the sentence with a negative characteristic that contrasts with the positive characteristic in *italics*.

corrupt	dishonest	uncommitted
cowardice	reviled	violent
cruel	self-centred	

1. A hero is *peaceful* and tries to solve problems without fighting. A villain is _____, often aggressive, and likes to fight.
2. A hero is *kind* and helps those in need. A villain is _____ and is mean and hurtful to others.
3. A hero is *well-respected* and liked by many people. A villain is _____ by most people, who think he is a bad character.

4. A hero is *selfless* and will sacrifice his own needs for the good of others. A villain is _____ and is concerned only with his own well-being.

5. A hero is *dedicated* and faithful to his cause. A villain is _____ and doesn't remain loyal to a cause.

6. A hero is *trustworthy* and can be depended on to do the right thing. A villain is _____ and can't be depended on because he is dishonest and fraudulent.

7. A hero is *honest* and will tell the truth. A villain is _____ and will tell lies.

8. A hero will *show courage* when he has to fight evil. A villain might show _____ and run away from a tough challenge.

Exercise D

Write the negative characteristic that best describes the following behaviours in the blanks.

1. He extorts money from all the shopkeepers on the street. Each week he forces them to pay him $100 in protection money so their shops will be safe. He is _____.

2. He hurts people unnecessarily just for the fun of it. He is _____.

3. He is never concerned about how his actions might affect others. He always puts himself first and does things only if they directly benefit him. He is _____.

4. You should never believe anything that he tells you because he lies all the time. He is _____.

5. When he was faced with a situation that was dangerous and he thought he might be harmed, he took off fast. He displayed _____.

6. He is cruel to everyone and has hurt many people badly. He is _____.

7. He doesn't care about any particular cause and will not get involved. He is _____.

8. Others absolutely hate him because he is so violent and evil. He is _____.

Grammar Focus

Adverbs of Manner

Exercise A

Look at the following sentences. Circle the word in each sentence that indicates **how** something happened or was done.

1. Terry Fox ran 42 kilometres a day consistently during his Marathon of Hope. _____

2. Helen Keller worked tirelessly to improve working and living conditions for the blind. _____

3. Incredibly, Lance Armstrong won the Tour de France after beating cancer. _____

4. Frederick Banting researched determinedly to discover a treatment for diabetes. _____

5. Greg Mortensen risked his life continuously to build schools for the children in the western Himalayas. _____

6. Nhat Hanh focused his efforts steadfastly on rebuilding destroyed villages during the Vietnam War. _____

7. Pelé, Brazil's greatest soccer player, played skilfully to win three World Cups. _____

8. Irena Sendlerowa, a social worker in Poland, was unwaveringly determined to save children from the Jewish Ghetto. _____

9. David Suzuki has purposefully worked for years to educate people about living in balance with nature. _____

10. Michael Phelps swam speedily to win eight gold medals in the 2008 Beijing Olympic Games. _____

Exercise B

Adverbs of manner can be placed in several different positions in the sentence, depending on the purpose of the adverb. They can be:

a) placed after the verb to describe how the action or activity was performed;

b) placed after a transitive verb + object to emphasize how the action was performed;

c) placed between the auxiliary verb and main verb to describe how the action or activity was performed;

d) placed before the adjective to modify the quality or character of the adjective; or

e) placed at the beginning of a sentence with a comma to express the attitude of the writer or speaker toward the sentence it modifies.

Look at each sentence in Exercise A and determine the position of the adverb of manner. Write the letter of the corresponding pattern on the line after each sentence.

For each pattern from Exercise B, write your own sentence.

Which sentence pattern is the most common? The second-most common?

Exercise C

Adjectives are used to describe a noun. An adverb of manner describes how a person performs an action or activity. Rewrite each sentence using an adverb of manner to describe the person's performance.

Example: She is a tireless volunteer. <u>She volunteers tirelessly every Friday evening</u>.

He is a knowledgeable art collector. <u>He speaks knowledgeably about art</u>.

1. He is a careful driver.
___

2. She is an excellent teacher.
___

3. She is a graceful dancer.
___

4. He is an eager student.
___

5. She is a silent reader.
___

6. He is a proud firefighter.
___

7. She is a natural skater.
___

8. He is a defensive player.
___

Grammar Edit

The following story about a real-life hero was submitted to a heroes website. Before the site administrator could share the story on the website, he had to make five changes to correct adverb mistakes. Underline each error and write the correct form of the adverb above it.

When I think of heroes, I think of individuals who have sacrificed everything so that the people in their country can be free. One of my heroes is Aung San Suu Kyi. Her father was a national hero who
5 brave fought to free Burma from British domination. She followed in his footsteps determined fighting the military regime that took over after the British left. She was democratic elected and should be the prime minister of Myanmar (formerly called Burma), but
10 the powerful military unlawful refused to recognize the vote. They thought that she was a threat to their power and placed her under house arrest. She was famous awarded the Nobel Peace Prize for her non-violent struggles for freedom. She is a freedom fighter
15 who has never given up her beliefs or resorted to violence in her fight for democracy—that's why she is my hero.

Reading

Guided Summary

A summary is a short, concise piece of writing that requires you to put the main points of the reading in your own words. It is always shorter than the original reading.

Complete this summary of the reading in the Student Book, pages 3–5. You will need to write more than one word in some of the blanks.

A woman and her baby _____.
They _____ by Superman.
Superheroes _____ because
of _____. They make
personal _____ to save
others from _____. Their
amazing skills come from different sources. Some
superheroes _____ with
their powers. Some got their powers as a result of
_____. Some are actually
_____. Other superheroes
create and use _____
to fight the bad guys. Superheroes have
_____ with which we identify.
Often they live like _____
in our society. We can easily relate to this second
identity. Kids today see superheroes when they go
_____. Computer special
effects let everyone's imagination come to life. We can
see our favourite _____ fighting
evil. The movies remind us of simpler times when
good would win _____.

Writing

Model Paragraph

Although I think of myself as an ordinary person, last year I became a hero for a short while. I was walking home from the subway at about 2:00 a.m. on a frosty Saturday morning. I was looking up the street to see
5 if anyone else was around when I saw small flames shooting out the roof of my neighbour's house. I grabbed my cellphone out of my purse and called the emergency number. As I was running the half block to the burning house, I gave the operator the location
10 of the fire. I reached the house and started pounding furiously on the door and yelling, "Fire! Fire!" All the noise I was making woke up my neighbours. They grabbed their sleeping children and ran out of the house in their pajamas and bare feet. Within minutes
15 the fire trucks arrived and dozens of firefighters battled the blaze that had spread to the second floor where my neighbours had been sleeping just a short time before. Later, the firemen told me that my quick reaction had saved my neighbours' lives. That night I was a hero.

1. What story is the writer trying to tell?
2. Who is the story about? When did it happen? What happened in the story?
3. How is the information in the story ordered?
4. What transitional expressions are used to signal the order of events?
5. Is there any information in the story that does not support the main idea?

> **Narrative Paragraphs**
>
> The narrative paragraph tells a story, which explains something. It makes the reader feel involved in the story or have an emotional reaction to it. It describes important details such as who is involved, where the story takes place, when, why and how it happens. An effective narrative paragraph is ordered chronologically.

Exercise A

Put the following sentences in chronological order so the story makes sense. Write the order number on the line at the beginning of the sentences.

___ a) My mom bought me a Superman lunch pail when I began school, but she wouldn't let me wear my Superman pajamas. She said I should go dressed as Clark Kent so no one would know that I was a superhero.

___ b) My mother rushed me to the hospital where a doctor put my leg in a cast.

___ c) My superhero days came to a fast end one day when I was six. I was playing at home. With my red cape tied securely around my neck, I jumped from the roof of our garage.

___ d) From the age of four, I watched Superman on TV every Saturday morning starting at 6:00 a.m. When my parents got up, I would be sitting in front of the TV in my Superman pajamas—eyes glued to the cartoons.

___ e) I had broken my leg.

___ f) Alas, my superhero days were over!

___ g) Every day when I got home from school, I would tie a red tablecloth around my neck and pretend I was the "caped crusader." I pretended that I could see through things with my X-ray vision.

___ h) I was very surprised that I did not fly. I fell to the ground in a crumpled pile.

Create a topic sentence for this paragraph, one that clearly prepares the reader for what follows.

_____

_____

Exercise B

Create your own exciting story where you are the hero. Answer the following questions by circling the words that describe your imagined actions.

1. When did your heroic event occur?

   I became a hero (*a few / several / many*) (*years / months / days*) ago.

2. Where were you? What happened?

   I was at (*school / work / the mall*). I heard (*someone yell / alarms sounding / a gunshot*).

3. How did you react?

   I (*looked to see what was going on / ran to help / ran for the nearest exit*).

4. What happened next?

   I saw (*an upset woman in a black dress / someone wearing a mask / a man who was out of breath*) carrying (*an oversized bag / a weapon / a small child*) (*in his (her) arms / over his (her) shoulder / in his (her) right hand*) running. (*She / He*) ran (*down the stairs / into the crowd that had gathered / around the corner*).

5. What did you do when that happened?

   I (*yelled, "Stop!" / chased after the person / used my cellphone to call the police*). Then I (*shouted "Grab him (her)" / grabbed the person's arm / told the police officer what I had seen*).

6. What happened next?

   Moments later the (*man (woman) disappeared from sight / turned toward me / stopped*). Then (*he / she*) (*cried "Help my baby! My baby is choking!" / pointed the gun at me / ran for the exit*). I (*grabbed the infant, turned her over, thumped her on her back, and got her breathing / karate chopped him (her) on the arm and he (she) dropped the gun / told the police where he (she) had gone*). Because of my actions (*the distraught man (woman) / the thief / the police*) (*was / were*) (*helped / caught / given a clear description*).

7. How did that make you feel?

   Helping (*save the baby / catch the thief / the police*) was the (*most exciting / scariest / bravest*) thing I have ever done.

Fill in the gaps in this paragraph with information about what you did or imagined you would do if there were an emergency.

I became a hero _____ _____ ago.

I was at _____ when I heard _____. I knew that I had to do something so I _____.

I saw that _____ was running, carrying _____ _____. _____ ran _____. I _____. Then I _____.

Moments later the _____. Then _____ _____. I _____.

Because of my actions, the _____ _____ _____.

Helping _____ was the _____ thing I have ever done.

Exercise C

For a story to be effective, it has to move smoothly from one action to another. Writers can use tenses to show the sequence of actions. They also use words such as the following to signal time order and to indicate when one action finishes and another action begins.

before	after	meanwhile
first	after a while	while
at first	soon	during
now	finally	today
next	when	yesterday
then	as soon as	last night
later	upon	

Read the narrative paragraph below. Fill in each blank with a word or phrase that makes sense. Try to use signal words only once.

1. _____ I was twelve years old, I read a really sad story in the newspaper. The article was about the murder of a young boy named Iqbal Masih. This young boy had been sold into slavery at the age of four. He spent the next six years of his short life chained to a carpet-weaving loom. 2. _____ he began to speak out for children's rights, but the media coverage he received angered some people who wanted him silenced. Iqbal was killed. This story inspired me because 3. _____ reading Iqbal's story, I realized that even someone young can change the world. 4. _____ I got my eleven-year-old friends to help me and I began my fight against child labour. 5. _____ I got more kids involved. I eventually involved thousands of young people around the world. 6. _____ I am the head of the worlds' largest network of children helping children through education. It includes youth in 45 countries. My name is Craig Kielburger and I am a social activist.

Exercise D

Use the following sequence of events to write a narrative paragraph. Add time words or expressions to make the sequence of events clear.

1. walk the dog
2. hear a scream
3. run to the river bank
4. see a child struggling in the water's fast current
5. grab a big stick
6. drag the child out of the water
7. cover the child with coat
8. call emergency rescue
9. told I saved the child's life

✔ Narrative Paragraph Checklist

Content
- [ ] Does my topic sentence tell the main point of my story?
- [ ] Have I chosen only the important events that relate to the main point of the story?
- [ ] Does my concluding sentence draw the reader's attention to the topic sentence again?

Organization
- [ ] Do I begin with one or two sentences that introduce the situation or background of the story?
- [ ] Have I organized the events in the paragraph in chronological order?

Meaning
- [ ] Have I used appropriate words or expressions to show time order?
- [ ] Have I used precise words to describe the events?
- [ ] Have I used tenses effectively to show time order?

Mechanics
- [ ] Have I checked my paragraph for mistakes in grammar, spelling, and punctuation?

Academic Word List

| alter | element | job | physical | series |
| attribute | generate | motivate | recover | source |

Word Meaning
Exercise A

Circle the word in parentheses that matches each of the following definitions.

1. to provoke someone to behave in a particular way (attribute / motivate / alter)
2. a daily or weekly TV program with the same people and format (job / element / series)
3. connected with a person's body (element / attribute / physical)
4. to produce or create something (generate / compute / alter)
5. the place something comes from (source / element / attribute)
6. to change or make different (recover / alter / compute)
7. work for which you receive regular payment (element / attribute / job)
8. one of the four substances: earth, air, fire, and water (element / physical / job)
9. to get well again after being hurt (alter / recover / compute)
10. a physical or personality characteristic of a person or thing (element / job / attribute)

Pronunciation
Exercise B

Listen to your teacher or an audio dictionary to hear the pronunciation of each word in the list. Repeat each word aloud. Mark the syllables and major word stress.

1. alter (v)   ăl / ter
2. attribute (n) _____
3. element (n) _____
4. generate (v) _____
5. job (n) _____
6. motivate (v) _____
7. physical (adj) _____
8. recover (v) _____
9. series (n) _____
10. source (n) _____

Word Forms
Exercise C

Fill in the blank with the word form shown in parentheses. Select only word forms that have the same meaning as in Exercise A.

1. alter (v): _____ (adj)
   _____ (n)
   _____ (adj)
2. attribute (n): _____ (n)
   _____ (v)
3. element (n): _____ (adj)
4. generate (v): _____ (n)
   _____ (adj)
5. job (n): _____ (adj–neg)
6. motivate (v): _____ (n)
   _____ (n)
   _____ (adj)
   _____ (adj)
   _____ (adj)
7. physical (adj): _____ (adv)
   _____ (n)
8. recover (v): _____ (adj)
   _____ (n)
9. series (n): _____ (adj)
10. source (n): _____ (v)

Exercise D

In a dictionary, find one example sentence for each word in Exercise A and copy it into your notebook. Write a second sentence of your own. Then, work with a partner to revise and edit your sentences.

Vocabulary in Context
Exercise E
Read the following paragraph and complete each blank with one of the words from the list below. Use each word only once.

alter	generated	physical	source
attributes	job	recover	
elements	motivated	series	

I think that paramedics are real-life heroes. One of my favourite TV ₁_____ is a reality show about the emergency calls that paramedics respond to. The paramedics' ₂_____ often involves personal risk because they never know what danger they may be walking into. Sometimes they are called to treat a person who has taken street drugs that ₃_____ the person's normal behaviour. The person could become dangerously violent at any time. The paramedics have to quickly assess the potential risk involved and decide if it is safe to approach the individual to offer assistance. Every time they approach an unknown situation, there is risk. They have to be very careful. They brave the ₄_____ to go to people's aid, often driving through terrible snowstorms and other bad weather. They are usually the first people on the scene and the first to provide medical attention. They have to quickly find the ₅_____ of the victim's problem and provide medical support until they can get the person to the hospital. Their job is very ₆_____. Often they may have to carry a large man on a stretcher down stairs to get him to the waiting ambulance. Consequently, strength and fitness are necessary ₇_____ of paramedics. They frequently injure their backs and have to take time off to ₈_____. It is a wonder that anyone wants such a dangerous job, but many paramedics are ₉_____ by the joy of helping others. They also like the excitement that is ₁₀_____ by not knowing what will happen each time they get a call. Not everyone has the heroic qualities needed to be a paramedic.

Unit 2
Ancient Secrets Revealed

Vocabulary

Exercise A
Complete the sentences with words from the list.

ancient	excavation	proof	society
archaeology	forgeries	reveal	speculation
code	hoax	rituals	theory
conspiracy	mystery	secret	

1. They cracked the special _____ and were able to understand the secret message.
2. Scientists use special techniques to _____ the approximate age of an artifact.
3. The _____ of how people were able to move huge stones without any machines remains.
4. They found many artifacts at the _____ site.
5. The bones are _____ that people lived in the area thousands of years ago.
6. Sometimes it is difficult to identify _____ if they are really good fakes.
7. _____ humans used animal bones to dig holes.
8. The _____ location of the gold has never been found.
9. Crop circles are a _____ according to some people. They are man-made, not made by aliens.
10. The _____ students are exploring the ancient ruins.
11. The artifacts tell us that the _____ that lived there was very advanced.
12. The druids had many _____ that they performed on the summer and winter solstice.
13. There is a lot of _____ but little proof as to how the huge stones were transported so many kilometres.
14. One _____ is that the workers used wooden rollers, ropes, and hundreds of men to move the large stones.
15. _____ theorists always think there is some big cover-up and we are not being told the truth.

Now, search for the words and circle them in the word grid. The words may be written horizontally, vertically, or diagonally, and can be written forwards or backwards. One example has been done for you.

```
    1  2  3  4  5  6  7  8  9 10 11 12
a   s  l  a  u  t  i  r  v  y  e  a  t
b   e  x  c  a  v  a  t  i  o  n  o  h
c   i  n  c  r  r  c  o  h  y  g  t  e
d   r  a  n  c  i  e  n  t  o  r  r  o
e   e  m  c  h  d  y  e  o  e  i  p  r
f   g  y  c  a  r  i  p  s  n  o  c  y
g   r  s  p  e  c  u  l  a  t  i  o  n
h   o  t  r  o  a  x  r  p  e  e  t  e
i   f  e  s  l  a  e  v  e  r  d  p  o
j   a  r  s  o  l  a  a  e  c  o  e  e
k   c  y  h  g  a  s  e  s  e  c  o  d
l   e  s  r  y  t  o  o  s  s  c  e  f
```

Exercise B
There are 15 words missing (^) in this text. Use your knowledge of sentence structure to identify the function of each missing word (noun, verb, etc.). Select an appropriate word from the list and write the answers in the column. Use each word only once.

code	speculation	conspiracy	ancient
rituals	proof	mystery	archaeology
society	reveal	hoax	excavation
secret	forgeries	theory	

The study of peoples and their cultures, which can include the ^ of long-forgotten cities, is called ^ People who are interested in finding out about an ^ civilization can read about the discoveries in the blogs of archaeologists. They used to keep their discoveries a ^ because they didn't want others to come to the site before they had uncovered enough ^ to clearly support their ^ of who lived there in ancient times. Of course not all finds are real. Some are in fact skillful ^ that some dishonest person has "discovered" in hopes of becoming famous or rich. Careful scientific examinations sometimes ^ that someone has tried to pull an elaborate ^ on the public. Because of this planned fraud, there is always ^ about the validity of any new claim when something amazing is discovered. There is still a lot of ^ associated with the ancient pyramids of Egypt. We can speculate about some of the ^ performed in the pyramids. Do the members of the secret ^ of the Freemasons know the pyramids' secrets? They are all sworn to a ^ of silence and are not allowed to tell anyone what they actually know. Some people believe that there is a ^ by the Freemasons to rule the world with the secret knowledge and wealth they have acquired.	(n) excavation

Grammar Focus

Past Time
Exercise A
Complete the following sentences with the simple past or past progressive form of the verb.

1. No one knows who _____ (create) the Nazca lines or why.

2. Unknown people _____ (make) 1000 lines and objects over an area of 1036 square kilometres.

3. It is a mystery who _____ (construct) a pictogram of a pelican that is five times larger than a jumbo jet.

4. Some scientists believe that the Nazca people _____ (use) two sticks with a string to create the long straight lines in some drawings.

5. The Nazca people _____ (not able) to view their work from above.

6. In the 1920s, while a commercial aircraft _____ (fly) over the region, passengers _____ (rediscover) the lines.

7. In 1968, Swiss explorer Erich von Daniken _____ (propose) that aliens had made the lines.

8. Some people believed that while aliens _____ (land) their spaceships, they _____ (use) the pictograms for navigation.

9. Someone _____ (pile) stones along the edge of the lines to make them clearer.

10. Some ancient civilizations _____ (believe) the sun and the moon were eyes of gods that _____ (live) in the sky and _____ (look) down on Earth.

Exercise B
Use the clues to write the dialogue. Use appropriate verb tenses and add any necessary missing words.

Example: Salim: do / know / there / be / Brazilian Stonehenge?

 Xian: Brazilian archaeologists / discover / 127 granite stone observatory / 2006.

 Salim: Did you know there is a Brazilian Stonehenge?

 Xian: Yes, Brazilian archaeologists discovered the 127 granite stone observatory in 2006.

San Agustin

SAN AGUSTIN

Kira: visit / San Agustin / go / Colombia / last summer?
Manjit: be / amazing

Kira: see / giant stone statues?
Manjit: have / terrifying faces. look / part human / part jaguar.

Kira: hear / be / largest group of megalithic statues / South America.
Manjit: that / what / tour guide / tell us.

Kira: Many / be / next to / burial sites / be not / they?
Manjit: 1913 / German archaeologist / Konrad Theodor Preuss / discover / tombs / contain / people / bury / with / lots / gold / silver.

Kira: be / statues / build / protect / tombs?
Manjit: That / be / what / many people / believe.

Kira: Who / build / statues?
Manjit: Experts / believe / people / ancient civilization / build / then / disappear / before / Europeans / arrive / 1500s.

> If the subject of the while clause is the same as the subject in the independent clause, *while* can be followed by V$_{ing}$.

Exercise C

Combine the following pairs of cues to make sentences with *while*.

Example:
a) Freemasons / live / communal lodge
b) build / cathedral

Freemasons lived in a communal lodge while they were building the cathedral.

OR

Freemasons lived in a communal lodge while building the cathedral.

1. a) Knights Templar / keep / people's money safe
   b) travel / Holy Land.

2. a) farmer / claim / find / Ica stones
   b) explore / local caves.

3. a) Strange patterns / appear in / farmer's field
   b) he / sleep.

4. a) team / discover / pieces / marble statue
   b) dig / ancient city.

5. a) man / find / mastodon bones
   b) dig / ditch / uncle's farm.

6. a) woman / find / fossilized bones
   b) clean / attic.

7. a) Ash / bury / thousands / people alive
   b) flee / volcano.

8. a) Archaeologists / discover / human remains
   b) excavate / ruins.

9. a) Ninjas / slow / their breathing
   b) wait / victim / sleep.

10. a) Ninjas / drip / poison / down string / into / victim's mouth
    b) sleep.

Grammar Edit

The following story about an ancient treasure was submitted to a magazine. There are 10 tense mistakes that the editor had to correct before the story could be printed. Underline the tense errors and write the correct form of the verb above it.

The police were arresting a farmer in a small village outside of Rome when they discovered ancient treasures hidden in his house. The archaeological police become suspicious a few weeks earlier when they were seeing fresh piles of dirt next to the river. While they investigated, they found small pieces of broken pottery. The police were watched the farmer digging for several days. When they were going to his house, they found more than 500 fragile miniature pots made approximately 2600 years ago. The jars were made between the seventh and fifth centuries BCE. The farmer breaking Italian laws by not reporting that he had found the ancient artifacts immediately to the authorities. That is why they arrested him.

Archaeologists believe that people living in the area throw the pottery into the river during festivities as offerings to deities. These pots were symbols of storage and cooking pots were using in daily life. Italy has very strict laws about individuals finding and keeping ancient artifacts. They make it a law years ago because at the time they wanted archaeologists to investigate these finds to learn more about the people from these ancient cultures.

Reading

Guided Summary

A summary is a short, concise piece of writing that requires you to put the main points of the reading in your own words. It is always shorter than the original reading.

Complete this summary of the readings on pages 19–20 of the Student Book. You will need to write more than one word in some of the blanks.

Japanese ninjas were _____ who lived _____. They used _____ to keep from being discovered so they _____ around easily. They trained _____ so they could stay still for days and they trained their eyes _____. They used _____ to kill silently. They passed _____ only to their _____.

Freemasons were skilled craftsman who built _____ in the late sixteenth century. They also knew about _____ of the buildings they constructed. There were many levels in the _____ and each level had secret _____. Churches didn't like that this organization was not _____. The Freemasons used _____ and _____ to protect their knowledge from others.

Writing

Model Paragraph

The Great Pyramid of Giza in Egypt and the Great Pyramid of Cholula in Mexico are both world famous monuments, but there are several significant differences between them. One major difference is the construction. The Great Pyramid of Giza was constructed following a single design over a period of 20 years. The Great Pyramid of Cholula, on the other hand, was constructed in four stages. Over 14 centuries, the pyramid was enlarged by constructing a new building around the first building, incorporating each previous structure into the next. The pyramids also differ in dimension. Giza is the tallest stone monument in the world with a height of 146.6 metres and a base of 230 by 230 metres. It is the shape of a true pyramid. The outside surface is made of smooth stones. In contrast, Cholula—the largest monument in the world and largest pyramid by volume—is only 66 metres in height with a base of 450 by 450 metres. It has a flat top with steps constructed on the outside.

20 The final major difference is the reason each structure was built. Giza was built as the burial place for the Egyptian Pharaoh Khufu and was not intended to be entered after his death. This differs from Cholula, which was built as a temple dedicated to the deity
25 Quetzalcóatl and used as a place for public ceremony and ritual. These two monuments, continents apart, are both famous pyramids with very different styles and purposes.

1. What is the writer's aim in this paragraph?
2. What is the topic of this paragraph? Underline the sentence that tells what this paragraph is about.
3. How does the writer organize the comparison points in relation to the topics being compared? Is the paragraph point-by-point or all about one, then all about the other?
4. What word(s) are used to show similarities and differences?
5. What words are used to signal transitions between comparison points?

Paragraphs That Compare and Contrast

Comparison-and-contrast paragraphs show similarities and differences between ideas, people, or things. To compare two things, you show how they are similar. To contrast two things, you show how they are different. The things being compared or contrasted must belong to the same group. For example, you can compare the similarities and differences in secret societies.

The purpose of writing such a paragraph is to persuade or inform the reader. For example, in a paragraph comparing ancient societies you might want to inform the reader that both secret societies have exclusive memberships and have many rituals that members must learn.

Exercise A

The sentences below express similarities and differences. In each sentence, circle the joining word(s) that show comparison or contrast. Then list the words you've circled. Highlight any punctuation that is used with the expression.

1. Both Mayan and Egyptian pyramids are made out of stone.
2. Mayan pyramids are made mainly out of rough stone, but Egyptian pyramids are made out of cut stone.
3. Egyptian pyramids were tombs for pharaohs whereas Mayan temples were places of worship.
4. Unlike Egyptian pyramids that were built outside major cities, Mayan pyramids were built in busy city centres.
5. The Egyptian pyramid in Giza is a world-famous monument. Likewise, the Mayan pyramid in Cholula is a world-famous monument.
6. Thousands of workers constructed the Mayan pyramid. Thousands of workers also constructed the Egyptian pyramid.
7. The interior of the Egyptian pyramid is different from the interior of the Mayan pyramid.
8. While Mayan pyramids were built for current use, Egyptian pyramids were built to last forever.
9. The inside of the Mayan pyramid, which is a pile of stone rubble, differs from the inside of the Egyptian pyramid, which is a small room.
10. Just as many tourists go to see the Mayan pyramid each year, thousands of tourists go to see the Egyptian pyramid.

The words used to signal comparison and contrast can be coordinating conjunctions, subordinating conjunctions or conjunctive adverbs. Depending on the placement of these words and their function, they require different punctuation. See Appendix pages 136–37 for an explanation.

Comparison Word(s)	Contrast Word(s)
both ... and	but
just as ... also	whereas, while, although, unlike
similarly, likewise	
	in contrast, on the one hand/ on the other hand
	is/are different from, differ(s) from

Exercise B

Antonio wants to visit a historic excavation, but he can't decide between the ruins of the ancient city of Pompeii, Italy, and the ancient city of Angkor, Cambodia. To help him decide, he lists what he knows about each ancient city:

Organize the two lists according to common points of comparison:

Pompeii	Angkor
• destroyed and completely buried by a volcanic eruption in 79 CE	• thousands of temples mostly in ruins located in Cambodia. Includes Angkor Wat, one of the most famous ruins in the world
• excavation began in 1748 and has continued in several different phases to the present	• Hindu empire built in the early twelfth century
• visited by more than 2 million people every year	• abandoned in the fifteenth century when attacked by Thai invaders
• city built mainly during the Augustan period (27 BCE to 14 CE)	• covered over by the thick jungle and rediscovered in 1860 by French explorer Henri Mouhot
• covered by a thick layer of ash and soil, rediscovered in 1599, and then again in 1738	• restoration process began in 1907 and continues to present day, with a brief work stoppage during the civil war in the 1970s
• Pompeii is the biggest tourist attraction in Italy.	• visited by up to a million people a year
• a partially excavated Roman city near Naples, Italy. Includes ruins of an amphitheatre, swimming pool, aqueduct, public baths, private houses, and businesses	• Angkor Wat is the largest religious monument in the world.

Point-by-point Comparison
Exercise C

One basic way to organize a comparison-and-contrast paragraph is to make *point-by-point comparisons*.

In this type of writing, you write about each comparative point from both perspectives before moving on to the next point. For example, if you were comparing the ruins of Pompeii with the ruins of Angkor you would pick two or three comparative points, such as location, building types, and reason the location was abandoned.

Use the information from Exercise B to complete the organizational chart.

Comparative Point 1	location
Pompeii	
Angkor	
Comparative Point 2	purposes for the types of buildings
Pompeii	
Angkor	all temples
Comparative Point 3	reasons locations abandoned
Pompeii	volcanic eruption
Angkor	

This type of organization is useful when organizing complex topics. Points are clearly made because the reader is able to see the similarities and differences immediately.

Block Method Comparison

Another way to organize information is to write about all the comparative points for one topic first and then to write about the same comparative points for the second topic. This is called the block method, or *all about one and then all about the other*.

Use the information from Exercise B to complete the organizational chart.

Details about Pompeii
Excavation history
excavation began in 1748 and has continued in several different phases to the present
Popularity
Rediscovery

Details about Angkor
Excavation history
Popularity
visited by up to 1 million people every year
Rediscovery

Exercise D

The topic sentence for a comparison-and-contrast essay indicates what is being compared or contrasted. The following patterns can be used for topic sentences.

- There are several (similarities / differences) between X and Y.
- X and Y are (similar / different) in many ways.
- X and Y have several things in common.
- A comparison between X and Y shows that…

Write a topic sentence for a paragraph comparing Pompeii and Angkor.

_____

Exercise E

The following sentence patterns can be used to link points of comparison.

Comparison:
- Both X and Y + verb
- X and Y are similar in that (they)…
- X is similar to Y in that they … / because
- X + verb. Likewise, Y + verb
- X + verb. Y also + verb
- Like X, Y + verb …

Contrast:
- Unlike X, Y + verb …
- X+ verb, but Y + verb
- X + verb whereas Y + verb
- X is different from Y in that they … / because
- X differs from Y because …
- While X + verb, Y + verb
- X is … On the other hand, Y is …

Use the different patterns to write comparison or contrast sentences for the points in Exercise C.

1. location: _____

_____

2. purpose of building: _____

_____

3. reason locations abandoned: _____

_____

4. excavation: _____

_____

5. popularity: _____

_____

6. rediscovery: _____

Exercise F

Using the information in Exercises B, C, and D, write a paragraph in which you compare Pompeii and Angkor. Use the Comparison-and-Contrast Paragraph Checklist to edit your work.

Exercise G

Draw a chart as in Exercise B, comparing two subjects of your choice. Exchange your chart with a classmate and write a comparison-and-contrast paragraph based on the information in your classmate's chart. Use the Comparison-and-Contrast Paragraph Checklist to edit your work.

✔ Comparison-and-Contrast Paragraph Checklist

Content

☐ Does my topic sentence state what my paragraph is about?

☐ Is it clear that my purpose is to explain, to persuade, or to inform?

☐ Do I use the most significant comparative and contrasting points to support the main point in my topic sentence?

☐ Do I use the same comparative and contrasting points for each item?

☐ Do all my statements connect to my perspective on the topic?

☐ Does my concluding sentence draw the reader's attention to the topic sentence again?

Organization

☐ Is the information in the paragraph organized in either by a point-by-point or block method?

Meaning

☐ Have I used appropriate words to show similarities and differences?

☐ Have I used precise words to communicate my meaning?

Mechanics

☐ Have I checked my paragraph for mistakes in grammar, spelling, and punctuation?

Academic Word List

consequently	evidence	projects
construction	expert	require
designers	identity	
ethnic	professional	

Word Meaning

Exercise A

Choose the answer that has the same meaning as the bolded word in each sentence.

1. You have to be a member to learn the secrets of the organization. **Consequently**, non-members don't really understand how the organization works.

   a) as a result b) next in order c) in addition

2. The **construction** of the pyramids took decades and thousands of workers.

   a) design b) engineering c) building

3. The **designers** of the pyramids put them in a pattern with the stars.

   a) builders b) plan creators c) owners

4. Freemasons did not all have the same **ethnic** backgrounds as they came from many different countries with unique customs.

   a) sharing a distinct cultural background b) sharing physical characteristics c) sharing a common language

5. Archeologists have uncovered **evidence** that pharaohs were buried with great treasures.

   a) beliefs b) proof c) artifacts

6. The freemasons were **expert** in their different building skills.
   a) well paid b) somewhat knowledgeable
   c) specialists

7. The secret society members had special signals to help **identify** themselves to other members of the society.
   a) mislead b) hide c) reveal

8. She is very **professional** at work and always does her job competently.
   a) educated b) skillful c) recognized

9. He has been hired to complete several large **projects** by the end of the year.
   a) planned tasks b) art sketches c) objects

10. Construction of a pyramid **requires** great skill and precision.
    a) provides b) teaches c) needs

Pronunciation
Exercise B

Listen to your teacher or an audio dictionary to hear the pronunciation of each word in the list. Repeat each word aloud. Mark the syllables and major word stress.

1. consequently (adv):   còn / se / quent / ly
2. construction (n):   _____
3. designers (n):   _____
4. ethnic (adj):   _____
5. evidence (n):   _____
6. expert (n):   _____
7. identify (v):   _____
8. professional (adj):   _____
9. projects (n):   _____
10. require (v):   _____

Word Forms
Exercise C

Fill in the blank with the word form shown in parentheses. Select only word forms that have the same meaning as in Exercise A.

1. consequently (adv): _____ (adj)
   _____ (adj)
2. construction (n): _____ (v)
3. designers (n): _____ (v)
   _____ (adj)
   _____ (n)
4. ethnic (adj): _____ (adv)
   _____ (n)
5. evidence (n): _____ (adj)
   _____ (adv)
6. expert (n): _____ (adv)
   _____ (n)
7. identify (v): _____ (adj)
   _____ (n)
8. professional (adj): _____ (n)
   _____ (n)
   _____ (adv)
9. projects (n): _____ (v)
10. require (v): _____ (n)
    _____ (adj)

Exercise D

In a dictionary, find one example sentence for each word in Exercise A and copy it into your notebook. Write a second sentence of your own. Then work with a partner to revise and edit your sentences.

Vocabulary in Context
Exercise E

Read the following paragraph and complete each blank with one of the words from the list. Use each word only once.

consequently	evidence	projects
construction	expert	require
designers	identify	
ethnic	professional	

Did you know that they started ₁_____ on the new condo on my street? Before building there, they hired an ₂_____ in feng shui to ₃_____ where to position the building in relation to nearby water and alignment with the stars so the building would have good luck. I don't know if there is actually any 4_____ that it makes any difference. However, there are certain 5_____ groups that really believe that if you follow the guidelines of feng shui, you will have good fortune. 6_____, those builders who don't do this sometimes have trouble renting or selling their units. Many people hire 7_____ who specialize in feng shui decor to ensure that the layout of their home allows negative energy to exit. Achieving an appropriate flow of positive and negative energy may 8_____ the homeowner to hang mirrors in strategic locations to send bad energy out. My friend is a 9_____ designer who really believes in feng shui. She has been hired as a feng shui expert to give her advice on many 10_____. She credits her ability to apply the principles of feng shui with her phenomenal success in the industry.

Unit 3
O Canada, *Je t'aime*

Vocabulary

Exercise A

Match the examples with the word from the list that best categorizes them.

arctic	landscapes	provinces
borders	Maritimes	regions
coasts	mountains	territories
flatlands	natural resources	tundra
forests	Prairie	valleys

1. Ontario, Alberta, Nova Scotia _____

2. Nova Scotia, Prince Edward Island, New Brunswick _____

3. Alberta, Saskatchewan, Manitoba _____ provinces

4. west edge of Vancouver, outer edge of PEI, eastern edge of New Brunswick _____

5. Yukon, Nunavut _____

6. The Rockies, Mont Tremblant, Snow Dome _____

7. oil, gold, trees _____

8. hectares of deciduous trees, hectares of coniferous trees _____

9. the Saint Lawrence River, Okanagan in BC, the Red River _____

10. permafrost areas of northern Canada, Russia, and Greenland _____

11. the ocean at the northern most point of the earth, the region at the northern most part of the earth _____

12. Great Plains, eastern Alberta, much of Saskatchewan _____

13. intersection of Alberta and Saskatchewan, place where Yukon meets the NWT _____

14. six geographical _____ of Canada: the Atlantic provinces, the Canadian Shield, the North, the Plains, the Cordillera, and the Great Lakes–St. Lawrence area

15. a picture of the grain elevators in Saskatchewan, a photo of the majestic Rocky mountains, a painting of a pristine lake in Northern Canada _____

Exercise B

Fill in the missing consonants to spell the missing words. Use the map on page 24 of the Student Book to follow the trip.

It is my dream to take a extended trip across Canada. I want to visit all ten ₁_ _ o_ i_ _ e _ and three ₂ _ e _ _ i _ o _ ie _. I live in Newfoundland, so I plan to take the ferry across to Nova Scotia. I really want to go to Cape Breton Island and drive along the Cabot Trail. If I plan it well, I should be able to enjoy some spectacular hiking and see whales swimming off the ₃ _oa _ _. I'm going to take another ferry across to PEI. I hope to visit all 27 lighthouses and, of course, Green Gables, the home of Anne Shirley. Then, I'll take the Confederation Bridge across to the remaining ₄ _ a _ i _ i _ e province, New Brunswick. Apparently the drive across the bridge takes ten minutes. It's a very long bridge! I definitely want to see the Bay of Fundy because it has some of the highest tides in the world. The water level can change up to 13 metres within a few hours. Since 80 percent of New Brunswick is covered in ₅ _o_e_ _, I imagine the drive to Quebec might get a little boring, driving through kilometre after kilometre of trees. Once I get to Quebec, I'll have to practise my French. I've heard the best way to see Old Quebec is in a horse-drawn carriage. There are also some great wine ₆ _e_io_ _ to visit. The area is known for its vineyards. From there, I'll continue to Ontario, a province rich in ₇ _a_u_a_ _e_ou_ _e_ such as gold and copper. There I'll visit the capital city of Canada—Ottawa. If I take the Trans-Canada Highway across the ₈ _ _ ai_ ie provinces of Manitoba and Saskatchewan, I could be spending several days driving across the ₉ _ _ a _ _ a _ _ _. I'll be driving many hours on some of the flattest land in Canada. That will be a sharp contrast to the amazing ₁₀ _a_ _ _ _a _e _ I'll see from the scenic train ride that will take me from Alberta to British Columbia across the majestic Rocky ₁₁ _ou_ _ai_ s. The Rockies are even higher than the Alps. Some of the best Canadian wines are produced in the Okanagan ₁₂ _a_ _e_ in BC with beautiful views of surrounding hills and mountains. I'll spend a few days touring the different vineyards there. Then I'll head north. British Columbia ₁₃ _o_ _e_ _ both the Yukon and the Northwest Territories. I don't want to miss Dawson City, the Yukon town famous for the Klondike gold rush in 1897. If the weather is good, I could drive to Inuvik in the Far North. It's actually located two degrees above the ₁₄ A_ _ _i_ Circle. Crossing the frozen ₁₅ _u_ _ _a of the northern Territories will be incredible. Who knows, maybe I'll even get to cross part of the region by dog sled. Alternatively, I could fly from Yellowknife to Iqaluit. If I'm lucky, maybe I'll get to see the aurora borealis—an amazing natural light display in the sky. After that, I'll go back home to Newfoundland with amazing memories of my epic cross-Canada adventure.

Grammar Focus

Quantifiers

Exercise A

Complete the information about Canada by filling in the blanks with quantifiers that can be substituted for the word / expression in parentheses.

1. _____ (millions of) Canadians watch the hockey games to see who will win the Stanley Cup.

2. In _____ (just about all) areas of Canada there are four distinctive seasons.

3. _____ (includes all members of the group) province and territory has a capital city.

4. Canada has _____ (in greater quantity) lakes and inland waterways than any other country and the longest coast line in the world.

5. _____ (every single member of a group) province and territory has an official flower and flag.

6. You can take a ferry to Newfoundland from _____ (one or the other of two) New Brunswick or Nova Scotia.

7. _____ (unspecified number) of Canada's natural resources include iron ore, nickel, zinc, copper, gold, lead, molybdenum, potash, diamonds, silver, fish, timber, wildlife, coal, petroleum, natural gas, and water.

8. _____ (an amount that is not exact—more than some but fewer than many) great inventions including basketball, the electric light bulb, the electric range, the electron microscope, standard time, the telephone, and the zipper were invented in Canada.

9. In the winter _____ (one and the other) snowmobiling and skiing are popular.

10. _____ (not many) people live in the Arctic where living conditions are harsh.

Exercise B

Circle the correct word to complete this conversation.

A: Have you done ₁ *many*/*much* skiing this year?

B: No, unfortunately there has been ₂ *little/a little* snow, so the ski hills aren't open.
A: Oh, that's too bad. Do you usually ski a lot?
B: I went ₃ *few/a few* times last year. We had a lot of snow last year.
A: Do ₄ *many/much* of your friends ski?
B: Yes. Most of my friends ski. In fact, very ₅ *few/a few* people that I know don't participate in at least one winter sport. All of my friends love the winter.
A: Do you participate in ₆ *many/much* other sports?
B: Yes. I snowshoe and play hockey. I have also done ₇ *little/a little* snowboarding, but I'm not very good at it. How about you?
A: Me? No way! I don't like the cold. I try to spend ₈ *little/a little* time outdoors in the winter. I'd much rather curl up with a good book in my warm apartment.

Exercise C

Use a quantifier to respond to the following questions.

1. Approximately how much of New Brunswick is forested? (75 percent)
   Approximately three-quarters of New Brunswick is forested.

2. What do Toronto and Ottawa have in common? (capital city)
   _____

3. Where does the largest percentage of Canadians live? (close to the US border)
   _____

4. Which province has a bigger population: Alberta or Ontario? (Ontario)
   _____

5. How many provinces have their own provincial flags? (100 percent)
   _____

6. Approximately how many people live in the Arctic? (not many at all)
   _____

7. How many adult Canadians know the words to "O Canada"? (every one of them)
   _____

8. Does Nova Scotia or PEI have tundra? (no)

Grammar Edit

Read through the paragraph. Underline the 10 mistakes in the use of quantifiers or the corresponding verb form. Write the correct word above it. The verb must agree with the subject in number.

The Canadian Rockies are part of the North American Rocky Mountain range. The Rockies cover parts of each Alberta and British Columbia. Much of the Canadian Rockies are composed of layered
5 sedimentary rock such as limestone and shale. There is several national parks in the Rockies, including Jasper, Banff, Kootenay, Yoho, and Waterton. Four of these national parks and three provincial parks are UNESCO World Heritage sites. Many of the mountain
10 range is protected by the parks. The mountains are a popular tourist destination. A few people fail to be impressed by the natural beauty of the Rockies—it's impossible not to be wowed. If you like to hike and camp, there is some alpine huts throughout the
15 Rockies where you can sleep or have a rest. There are most rivers and lakes where you can fish. Every year, a little adventurers attempt to climb Mount Robson and Mount Columbia. Outdoor enthusiasts go there to neither ski or snowboard on the majestic slopes. Many
20 people takes the two-day scenic train ride through the Canadian Rockies every year.

Reading

Guided Summary

A summary is a short, concise piece of writing that requires you to put the main points of the reading in your own words. It is always shorter than the original reading. The snapshots found on pages 25–27 of the Student Book are summaries of the important details about Canada's regions. Use the following chart to visually summarize key words that capture the information from the five snapshots.

	People	Geology	Climate	Industry
The North				
Pacific Coast				
The Prairies				
Central Canada				
The Atlantic Coast				

Note: The snapshots provide a general picture only and do not include detailed information about all the people living in the regions. See current census data for a complete breakdown.

Writing

Model Paragraph

The view from the **rocky** cliff where we have stopped for a rest while hiking is absolutely breathtaking. Below us, the mirror-like surface of the emerald green lake reflects the majestic pines that surround it. The ripples of small widening circles disrupt the smooth glassy surface as a **large** bird lands. The shoreline disappears into the thick growth of **tall** pine trees making it look as if the trees are rising out of the **cool** mountain waters. Rock cliffs border the ring of trees that encircle the calm waters. Leafy green bushes and towering **fragrant** pine trees erupt from surface cracks in the rocks—a living testament to the ability of a **tiny** seed to take root almost anywhere. Although the hike was difficult, getting this rare opportunity to see the best that Mother Nature can create is definitely worth it.

1. What is the writer's aim in this paragraph?

2. What is the topic of this paragraph? Underline the topic sentence.

3. What is the writer's point of view on this topic? Highlight the information that shows the writer's point of view on the topic.

4. Look at the bolded adjectives. What senses do they appeal to?

5. How is the description organized?
   a) General to Specific Information/Specific to General Information
   b) Small to Large/Large to Small
   c) Front to Back/Back to Front
   d) Centre to Outside/Outside to Centre

> **Descriptive Paragraphs**
>
> The descriptive paragraph describes a person, event, object, emotion, or scene. Specific words are used to create a clear and detailed image for readers. Descriptive paragraphs are very common in writing such as travel literature, science reports, police reports, and doctors' notes.
>
> Descriptive writing is often organized spatially. The writer first describes one part of a place and then moves logically to another part. The description may be from left to right, right to left, bottom to top, top to bottom, front to back, or back to front. Writers can also use order of importance to organize the paragraph. Usually the most important aspect is described first.

Exercise A

Word choice is very important when writing a descriptive paragraph because you are creating a picture with your words.

1. On a sheet of paper, create a chart with the following headings:

Nouns	Adjectives	Verbs	Adverbs

2. Imagine that you are *looking* at an apple and write down all the nouns, adjectives, and adverbs that you can think of. Use your dictionary.

3. Now *touch* the apple. Add nouns, adjectives, and verbs that you experience to your chart.

4. *Smell* the apple and add appropriate words to your chart.

5. *Taste* the apple. Include the nouns, adjectives,, and verbs you perceive.

6. *Listen* to the sound that you make as you eat the apple. Add appropriate words to your chart.

7. How does it make you *feel*? What *emotion* does it suggest? Add these words to your chart.

8. Write a paragraph describing your experiences of eating the apple.

9. Use the checklist on page 25 to edit your paragraph.

Exercise B

Read the following sentences. Underline the descriptive details (adjectives, verbs, adverbs, nouns) and identify what sense, emotion, or impression the details suggest.

Example: The <u>juicy green</u> apple on the <u>cluttered</u> kitchen counter <u>caught</u> my eye.

   touch, sight   sight   sight

1. An unmistakeable aroma of my favourite breakfast wafted from the kitchen.

2. Sweet golden maple syrup drips generously over the stack of steaming pancakes on the table.

3. A crystal vase holding five bright pink tulips decorates the breakfast table.

4. The morning news can be heard from the speakers strategically placed near the breakfast table.

5. The excited chirping of birds perched in the shady tree drifts in through the window.

6. The smell of freshly brewed coffee competes with the sweet smell of the pancakes for my attention.

7. I grasp the smooth, comfortable ceramic handle of my favourite mug and raise it to my lips.

8. I love the taste of strong dark-roast coffee first thing in the morning. It wakes me up.

Exercise C

Effective descriptive sentences use details that are concrete and specific to create a clear picture. The details stimulate our five senses—sight, smell, touch, taste, and sound—as well as our emotions and impressions. Rewrite the general sentences on the next page to describe the picture more specifically.

Exercise D

Underline the two prepositions and six prepositional phrases that show location / direction.

On one end of my coffee table sits a carving—an amazing gift I received last year from an artist friend from Yellowknife. The carving is of an Inuit hunter hunting a bear. It is made from Brazilian soapstone,
5 which has rich and varied shades of brown. The base of the statue is a rough, unfinished slab of soapstone. On the right, the hunter is ready to attack. In front of him, a large polar bear is trying to escape. The hunter is wearing a thick warm parka. His face is partially
10 hidden by the thick furry hood that surrounds his face. Below his parka you can see that he is wearing warm leggings made from animal skins. His feet, which are firmly planted on the rock, are covered in warm moccasin-like boots. Clutched in his right hand
15 is a roughly cut stick with a long thin sharpened stone tied to it like a hammer. The bear is leaning to the left as if it is trying to escape the hunter. Its enormous paws look as if they could kill the hunter with one single swipe. I think that the carving represents
20 survival. It is a real conversation starter for anyone visiting my house.

Exercise E

Effective descriptions are organized in a logical (usually spatial) order so the reader can create a clear picture in his or her mind.

- General to Specific Information / Specific to General Information
- Small to Large / Large to Small
- Front to Back / Back to Front
- Centre to Outside / Outside to Centre

Complete the description of the picture on the next page. The sentences are not in a logical order. Rearrange the sentences to describe the picture from the centre to the outside.

General	Specific
1. It's cold, but sunny.	1. It's a crisp, clear cold day with the sun shining brightly.
2. Some people are wearing warm clothes.	
3. They are skating.	
4. The ice is smooth.	
5. Music is playing from the speakers.	
6. You can hear children laughing.	
7. The ice rink is in front of some buildings.	
8. There is a round building surrounded by two tall buildings.	

above	between	on	surrounding
across	facing	on either	to the left
against	from	side (of)	(of)
along	in	on top (of)	to the right
around	inside	outside	(of)
at	in front (of)	over	under
behind	in the	supported	
below	middle (of)	by	
beneath	inside	surrounded	
beside	next to	by	

I took this snapshot at Hopewell Rock in New Brunswick. It shows the coolest thing we saw on our trip to the East Coast. It is a picture of the flowerpot rocks at low tide. During high tide, the bases of the rocks are surrounded by water and look like islands. But when the tide is out and the ocean floor is dry the rocks really do look like flower pots.

_____ a) I think the flowerpot rock on his left looks like the head of an alien.

_____ b) The chance to walk on the ocean floor is definitely something I won't forget.

_____ c) It's hard to imagine that within a few hours the tides will rise 10–13 metres and the area where people are walking will once more be under water.

_____ d) That's Jarod in the middle of the picture. He's actually standing on the ocean floor.

_____ e) The one on his right is much larger. It looks like it is about to tip over.

_____ f) That thin line below the horizon is the ocean; it's hundreds of metres away.

_____ g) This flat part that extends to the water is actually the mud of the ocean floor that gets exposed when the tide goes out.

_____ h) Check out the cool balsam fir and dwarf spruce trees growing on top.

Exercise F

The words in the box can be used to show location. Select an interesting picture and use appropriate words from the list to write six to eight sentences describing your picture.

☑ Descriptive Paragraph Checklist

Content

☐ Does my topic sentence focus on the dominant impression of what I am describing?

☐ Do all the ideas in the paragraph support the dominant impression of my description?

☐ Have I used precise and appropriate descriptive words (sight, sound, smell, taste, touch) to create clear and detailed pictures and impressions?

☐ Does my concluding sentence draw the reader's attention to the topic sentence again?

Organization

☐ Is the information in the paragraph organized in a logical order (generally spatial)?

- General to Specific Information/Specific to General Information
- Small to Large/Large to Small
- Front to Back/Back to Front
- Centre to Outside/Outside to Centre

Meaning

☐ Have I used appropriate words or expressions to show spatial relationships?

☐ Have I used precise words to communicate my meaning?

Mechanics

☐ Have I checked my paragraph for mistakes in grammar, spelling, and punctuation?

Academic Word List

area	expose	immigrants	reveal
brief	financial	major	
debate	range	participate	

Word Meaning
Exercise A

Match each underlined word or phrase from the sentences in Column A with the appropriate word in Column B.

Column A	Column B
1. The oil industry is a <u>very important</u> part of the economy in Alberta.	a) area
2. Soon, the artist will <u>make</u> his new painting <u>known</u> to the public.	b) brief
	c) debate
	d) expose
	e) financial
3. In Quebec, people will continue to <u>discuss opposing opinions</u> about separating from the rest of Canada.	f) range
	g) immigrants
4. This <u>region of the country</u> is known for its rich mineral deposits.	h) major
	i) participate
	j) reveal
5. Toronto is a popular destination for many <u>people who come from other countries</u> to live permanently in Canada.	
6. The light show in the northern sky known as the aurora borealis lasts for only a <u>short</u> time.	
7. That <u>group of mountains</u> is known as the Rockies.	
8. Many Canadians like to <u>take part</u> in outdoor activities such as tobogganing and skating.	
9. Attending post-secondary education in Canada is a large <u>money</u> commitment and many students must take loans to pay for this education.	
10. When the tide goes out, it will <u>show</u> the base of the flowerpot <u>that is usually hidden</u> under water	

Pronunciation
Exercise B

Listen to your teacher or an audio dictionary to hear the pronunciation of each word in the list. Repeat each word aloud. Mark the syllables and major word stress.

1. area (n)   à / re / a
2. brief (adj)   _____
3. debate (n)   _____
4. expose (v)   _____
5. financial (adj)   _____
6. range (n)   _____
7. immigrant (n)   _____
8. major (adj)   _____
9. participate (v)   _____
10. reveal (v)   _____

Word Forms
Exercise C

Fill in each blank with the word form shown in parentheses. Select only word forms that have the same meaning as in Exercise A.

1. area (n)
2. brief (adj): _____ (adv)
3. debate (n): _____ (v)
   _____ (adj)
4. expose (v): _____ (n)
   _____ (adj)
5. financial (adj): _____ (n)
   _____ (v)
6. range (n): _____ (v)
7. immigrant (n): _____ (adj)
   _____ (v)
   _____ (n)
8. major (adj): _____ (n)
   _____ (v)

9. participate (v): _____ (n)
   _____ (n)
   _____ (adj)
10. reveal (v): _____ (n)
    _____ (adj)

Exercise D
In a dictionary, find one example sentence for each word in Exercise A and copy it into your notebook. Write a second sentence of your own. Then, work with a partner to revise and edit your sentences.

Vocabulary in Context
Exercise E
Read the following paragraph and complete each blank with one of the words from the list. You do not have to change the grammatical form of any words. Use each word only once.

area	expose	immigrants	revealed
brief	financial	major	
debate	ranges	participate	

Choosing to move your entire family to a new country is a ₁_____ decision for families to make. ₂_____ often leave behind friends, family, and security. Many newcomers to Canada often settle in an ₃_____ where other people from their country are living. Toronto, Vancouver, and Montreal attract many people new to Canada. Obviously, few people would choose to move to isolated areas of Canada like the Yukon or the mountain ₄_____ in Cape Breton. Even if they live in a densely populated city, it can be very difficult for newcomers to find jobs. Many find themselves in ₅_____ hardship, which causes a lot of stress and worry for the new immigrants. As a result, sometimes their stay in a city like Toronto is ₆_____ because living downtown is very expensive and they may be able to find cheaper housing in the suburbs.

Once settled, it is important that newcomers try to ₇_____ in community events so they can learn about the culture and meet people in their neighbourhood. The best way to learn about and adapt to a new culture is to ₈_____ oneself to it as much as possible.

As a result of the challenges that many newcomers experience, there is an ongoing ₉_____ about Canada's immigration policy. This discussion has ₁₀_____ that more needs to be done to ensure that immigrants can succeed when they move here.

Unit 4
Stay Tuned!

Vocabulary

blog	features	media
celebrities	gaming	networking
communities	genre	texting
connect	hype	trend
devices	lurking	tweets

Exercise A

Read each selection. The underlined sentence parts and your knowledge of grammar will help you to complete the sentence with a word from the list.

1. The Internet *links computers together* so they can share information. This _____ of computers has revolutionized how people communicate.

2. Advances in communications and Internet technology lead to *changes in how people behave*. The first social-networking site began in 1997, but the _____ toward using online social networks didn't happen until about five years later.

3. Cellphone companies develop *new capabilities* for their products to make them more attractive to buyers. The companies improve the cellphones they make by adding new _____.

4. Electronic *gadgets* that allow people to communicate with others are improving at a very fast rate. The companies that make these machines spend a lot of money to improve their communication _____.

5. Emma is travelling through Asia. Her friends in Canada want to know all about her trip, so every week she *shares her experiences with many people on the Internet*. Emma has her own _____.

6. In online social-networking *groups*, members are *united by their shared interests*. Online social-networking groups are _____.

7. It is easy for people to *join together* with others through the Internet. The Internet makes it easy for people to _____.

8. New computer technology products are *advertised and discussed on television, radio, and the news all the time*. This _____ makes buyers want to buy the product before it arrives on the market.

9. *Playing video and computer games* is one of the most popular forms of entertainment. _____ is not only popular with teenagers. Adults love it too.

10. Reality TV has become a very popular *type of* television programming around the world. Surprisingly, sports is not a popular _____ of television programming.

11. Many parents are concerned about their children's safety online. They fear that adults who want to harm children *may secretly be watching* what is happening in the online communities where their children spend time. People think that _____ is an undesirable activity.

12. Today, people don't only get their news from the *newspaper, radio, or television*. They get their information from many different _____, including social-networking sites.

13. *Twitter* began in 2006 as a messaging service that allowed users to send and read *text messages of up to 140 characters*. Users can send and receive _____ through the Twitter website or through applications on mobile phones.

14. *Typing and sending messages using a cellphone* is more popular among youth than making a phone call. _____ is the most popular way to communicate over the phone.

15. Why are people so interested in the lives of *famous people*? People are fascinated with _____.

Exercise B

Complete the paragraph by filling in the blanks with words from the list in Exercise A. You may need to change the singular or plural form of the word. Use a word only once.

Want to know what your favourite 1_____ are doing—every minute of every day? Today's digital 2_____ make it easy. In the old days, newspapers, magazines, television, and radio created the 3_____ about the lives of the rich and famous. Today's computers and other portable electronic ₄_____ such as laptops and cellphones allow fans to follow every step of their favourite stars. Fans don't have to rely on magazines and tabloid newspapers to get the latest gossip about famous people anymore. Now, they can go to hundreds of different Internet sites and read about the superstars they love on ₅_____ written by professional stargazers. But you don't need to rely on professionals for your information. You can get lots of news from other fans or your own friends, using social ₆_____ sites. These sites create a ₇_____, where fans share a common interest and ₈_____ with others. Or, you can follow your pop-culture hero using a social-messaging service such as Twitter. Many stars ₉_____ daily to let their fans know what's up. Information technology companies are always improving or adding new ₁₀_____ to their programs, products, and services to attract new customers and satisfy their existing ones.

Vocabulary Expansion

Exercise C

Words are often partnered with other words. For example, it is common to speak or write about electronic media or media habits. Write words from the list beside the lines to make appropriate word partners. Many choices are possible. The lines to the left show that the word precedes the target word, and the lines to the right show that it follows the target word.

computer	global	mass	support
digital	gossip	mechanical	wireless
electronic	habits	online	worship
ethnic	hype	safety	
fashion	local	social	

1. ═══ media ───
2. ═══ device(s) ───
3. ═══ network(s) ───
4. ═══ community ───
5. ═══ celebrity(ies) ───
6. ═══ connection ───
7. ═══ trend(s) ───

Exercise D

Add partner words from Exercise C to fit the meaning of the sentence.

1. The movie actors who are famous in our home countries, may not be _____ celebrities. In other countries they may be unknown.

2. Today, many bands produce and distribute their music without big record companies. This _____ trend is possible because of the Internet.

3. Consumer electronics companies add new features to their _____ devices to attract new customers.

4. Without _____ support it's difficult for a recreation centre to stay open.

5. It is true that the _____ habits of youth have changed in the last few years, but it is not true that youth aren't watching television anymore.

6. Whether people have more online friends or more face-to-face friends is not important. The important thing is to have a good _____ network.

7. _____ media are only possible because of the Internet.

8. Many public buildings such as libraries offer users a free _____ *connection* to the Internet. Users don't need an Ethernet cable to plug into the Internet.

9. The _____ *hype* for new gaming systems is unbelievable.

10. Nowadays, fans can use social-networking, micro-messaging, and fan sites to check every detail of their favourite stars' lives. _____ *worship* is becoming more popular.

Grammar Focus

Reported Speech

Exercise A

What did the original speaker say? Change the reported speech into quoted speech.

1. Paul said that he didn't know how people could live without the Internet. _____

2. Lisa said that her mother was worried about how much time she spent online. _____

3. Tanja said that she wasn't worried about Internet safety. _____

4. The researchers said that the average age of computer- and video-game players was 35. _____

5. Jim said that he relies on the Internet to get the latest news. _____

6. Diego said that he puts a time limit on his kids' video-game playing. _____

7. David said that he was going to buy a new cellphone soon. _____

8. Jenny said that she thinks she's addicted to texting. _____

Exercise B

Underline the six reported speech sentences from the celebrity blog. Quote what the celebrity actually said.

The café where I interviewed glamour boy Rick Laguna was not the trendy hotspot you'd expect for a celebrity. The place was a greasy spoon—one of those places where thick dust sits on windowsills and your shoes
5 stick to the floor. Rick confided that he didn't follow the latest trends. He said he couldn't imagine spending more than $1.50 for a cup of coffee. He said that he didn't need twenty choices of coffee with latte, soy, or whipped cream. We sat for an hour. He talked about
10 his life as a child growing up in rural Nova Scotia where people told stories and looked out for each other. He admitted that he missed the small community where his parents and his sister still live. He lives in L.A. now. When the interview was over, he paid (usually
15 the interviewer does). I guess he can afford the three bucks. What surprised me, though, was that he left a $3 tip. He mentioned that before he became famous he had worked as a waiter. He said he had had to work hard for little pay. And that pretty much sums up this
20 superstar. He's a down-to-earth guy—simple, direct and kind. What you see is what you get.

_____
_____
_____
_____
_____
_____

Exercise C

Put the words in the proper order to make reported questions.

1. Do you read the newspaper?
   He asked I if the newspaper read.
   _____

2. Does she read entertainment blogs?
   He asked entertainment blogs if read she.
   _____

3. Do you have a cellphone contract?
   They asked a cellphone contract I if had.
   _____

30

4. How many text messages do they send and receive every day?
The researcher asked every day how many they sent and received text messages.
_____
_____

5. When did he stop playing video games?
His mother asked stopped playing when he video games.
_____
_____

6. Where did you buy that digital device?
His friend asked digital device bought he where that.
_____
_____

7. Who reads celebrity gossip blogs?
She asked celebrity gossip blogs read who.
_____
_____

8. How many friends are on your social-networking site?
She asked social-networking site friends on my how many were.
_____
_____

9. What online communities do you belong to?
The teacher asked belonged to what online communities we.
_____
_____

10. Why are social connections so important?
The professor asked so important were why social connections.
_____
_____

Exercise D

A media researcher interviewed a group of young adults about their media habits. Change the quoted speech questions into reported speech. Change pronouns and tenses as needed.

1. The interviewer asked the group, "How many hours per week do you spend playing computer games?"
_____
_____

2. The interviewer asked one young woman, "Do you have more face-to-face friends or more online friends?"
_____
_____

3. The interviewer asked the group, "Do you tweet?"
_____
_____

4. The interviewer asked one young man, "What genres of television programs do you like best?"
_____
_____

5. The interviewer asked one man, "What is your favourite online game?"
_____
_____

6. The interviewer asked one woman, "When do you go to sleep at night?"
_____
_____

7. The interviewer asked one woman, "Where do you get information about your favourite celebrity?"
_____
_____

8. The interviewer asked the group, "Do you listen to the radio?"
_____
_____

9. The interviewer asked one young woman, "Why do you prefer texting to calling?"
_____
_____

10. The interviewer asked the group, "Who are your favourite bloggers?"
_____
_____

Exercise E

The young adults in the research group answered the researcher's questions. The researcher reported their answers in a research report. Change the quoted speech into reported speech. Change pronouns and tenses as needed.

1. **Interviewer:** How many hours per week do you spend playing computer games? **Man:** About 20.

   Report: _____

2. **Interviewer:** Do you have more face-to-face friends or more online friends? **Young woman:** I have a lot more online friends.

   Report: _____

3. **Interviewer:** Do you tweet? **Young woman:** Yeah. I just started tweeting last week.

   Report: _____

4. **Interviewer:** What genres of television programs do you like best? **Young man:** I like drama shows.

   Report: _____

5. **Interviewer:** What is your favourite online game? **Young man:** I don't have one favourite game. I like several.

   Report: _____

6. **Interviewer:** On a weeknight, when do you go to sleep? **Young man:** Around midnight.

   Report: _____

7. **Interviewer:** Where do you get information about your favourite celebrities? **Woman:** From their websites.

   Report: _____

8. **Interviewer:** Do you listen to the radio? **Man:** Yeah, sometimes.

   Report: _____

9. **Interviewer:** Why do you prefer texting to calling? **Young woman:** Because it's cheaper.

   Report: _____

10. **Interviewer:** Who is your favourite blogger? **Woman:** I love Corey Doctorow's tech blog.

    Report: _____

Grammar Edit

A student is reporting what a blogger posted on his site. The student has made 10 errors in reporting what the blogger said:

5 *pronoun* errors
2 *that / if* errors
1 *reporting verb* error
2 *reporting question* errors

Find the mistakes and fix them.

₁Am I addicted to the Internet and my phone? ₂Last week I decided to write down how often I use my phone and the Internet. ₃During the week I read the news online while I ate breakfast. ₄I checked for personal voicemail or text messages on my cellphone on the way to work on the bus. ₅When I got to the office, I checked my phone messages. ₆Then I spent about half an hour reading and answering my work email. ₇Last week, I spent three hours of my day looking up information for work. ₈If no one is in the lunchroom when I eat my lunch, I check what my Facebook friends are doing. ₉Last week no one was in the lunchroom all week. ₁₀The bus ride home is boring so I always play a few games on my phone. ₁₁My wife called me on the way home on Friday. ₁₂She asked, "Do you want to go out for dinner?" ₁₃"Where do you want to go?" I asked. ₁₄We met at a little Italian restaurant. ₁₅During dinner I received three text messages and she made two phone calls.

₁The blogger asked that he was addicted to the Internet and his phone. ₂He reported that he decided to write down how often he used his phone and the Internet. ₃He said during the week he read the news online while I ate breakfast. ₄He said that he checked for personal voicemail or text messages on his cellphone on the way to work on the bus. ₅He said that when he got to the office, he checked his phone messages. ₆Then he spent about half an hour reading and answering my work email. ₇He reported that last week, I spent three hours of my day looking up information for work. ₈He asked if no one is in the lunchroom when he eats his lunch, he checks what his Facebook friends are doing. ₉He reported that last week no one was in the lunchroom all week. ₁₀He said if the bus ride home is boring so he always plays a few games on his phone. ₁₁The blogger said my wife called him on the way home on Friday. ₁₂She asked if do you want to go out for dinner? ₁₃He asked where did she want to go. ₁₄He said that they met at a little Italian restaurant. ₁₅He admitted that during dinner he received three text messages and she made two phone calls.

Reading

Guided Summary

A summary is a short, concise piece of writing that requires you to put the main points of the reading in your own words. It is always shorter than the original reading.

Complete this summary of the reading about teen media trends on pages 40–44 in the Student Book. More than one word may be necessary to communicate the idea.

People often think that teens do not use 1 _____ like radio and television anymore because they prefer new media. This is not true. Research tells us that teens use new media 2 _____ traditional media. 3 _____ is still the most common medium for teens. 4 _____ or 5 _____ programs are very popular with teenagers around the world. It is also not true that teens spend more time on computers than 6 _____. On the contrary, they spend 7 _____ on computers and the Internet than other age groups. In the United States, teens spend about 8 _____ as much time on the Web per month than the overall US 9 _____. It is also a myth that teens only 10 _____ with their cellphones now. Teens do text a lot, but they also use many different 11 _____. They download ringtones, games, and applications. They instant message and use the mobile Web. Finally, teens are also not the biggest 12 _____ of all age groups. Over the last two decades, the gaming audience has grown to include new groups of users, including 13 _____ _____. Overall, the research shows that the media habits of teens are 14 _____ from the media habits of 15 _____.

Writing

Model Paragraph

The amount of time teens spend using electronic media is endangering their physical and emotional health. A recent study by the Centre for Addiction and Mental Health shows that hundreds of thousands
5 of teens spend at least seven hours a day staring at a computer or TV screen. That's almost one third of an entire day. The problem is that when teens are sitting in front of a screen, they're not physically active. The study does not directly connect time spent in
10 front of a television or computer screen with poorer health, but experts like Dr. Robert Mann, the main researcher of the study, say it's no coincidence that teens' physical health is becoming worse. More than a quarter of the students in the survey said that they
15 were overweight or obese. Many students who spent long hours in front of a screen also said that they had had feelings of unhappiness and had lost sleep. Of course, all technology is not the same. Texting and writing long emails are social activities. They may
20 not have the same negative effects as playing some computer games. Still, researchers from other studies agree that parents have a good reason to be worried about how teens use media. The less time teens spend in front of the television or computer screen, the more
25 time they can spend going out with friends and being active. In short, less time in front of electronic screens means better overall health.

1. What is the writer's aim in this paragraph? What response does the writer want from the reader?
2. What is the topic of this paragraph? Underline the sentence that tells what this paragraph is about.
3. What is the writer's point of view on this topic? Highlight the information that shows the writer's point of view on the topic.
4. What kind of evidence is given to support the point of view stated in the topic sentence?

   a) **Facts:** knowledge that has been proven to be true by research
   b) **Statistics**: numbers—this also comes from research
   c) **Expert Opinion**: the opinions of experts—this comes from research.
   d) **Example:** from your own experience or from what you heard or read.
   e) **Common Sense**: things that you believe everybody knows.

> **Persuasive Paragraphs**
>
> The persuasive paragraph tries to convince the reader to agree with the writer's perspective on the topic. The writer's main point is stated in the topic sentence. In persuasive writing, the writer can use logic and emotion to convince the reader that his or her point of view on the topic is the truth. Persuasive writing is common in education, politics, business, and news reporting.

Exercise A

For each topic sentence, write out the topic and the point of view (controlling idea). You can review topic sentences on page 135 in the Appendix.

Example: North American youth have <u>too much</u> leisure time.
Topic: The leisure time of North American youth
Controlling idea: too much

1. Social-networking sites are dramatically changing our ideas of friendship.
Topic: _____
Controlling idea: _____

2. Traditional media will not survive in our digital world.
Topic: _____
Controlling idea: _____

3. Smart phones are making the computer unnecessary.
Topic: _____
Controlling idea: _____

4. The Internet improves reading skills.
Topic: _____
Controlling idea: _____

5. The Internet is responsible for our obsession with the daily lives of celebrities.
Topic: _____
Controlling idea: _____

6. Computers are making us lazy.
Topic: _____
Controlling idea: _____

7. Internet porn sites destroy young people's abilities to have healthy sexual relationships.
Topic: _____
Controlling idea: _____

8. The way people communicate online will change the way they communicate face-to-face.
Topic: _____
Controlling idea: _____

9. Today's online youth do not value privacy.
Topic: _____
Controlling idea: _____

10. The Internet generation is much more sophisticated than the generation before it.
Topic: _____
Controlling idea: _____

Exercise B

Use the guidelines for writing effective topic sentences to do the following:

a) Mark the effective topic sentences with a ✔ and the ineffective topic sentences with an ✘.
b) For the ineffective sentences, identify the problem.
c) Re-write the ineffective topic sentences to make them effective.

Topic sentences are ineffective if
a) the sentence simply states a fact;
b) the topic sentence in ungrammatical;
c) the topic sentence is too general; or
d) the topic sentence is too specific.

☐ 1. Teens are learning valuable skills when they're on the Internet.
_____

☐ 2. Spending time on the Internet brings families closer together.
_____

☐ 3. Teens around the world are the same.
_____

☐ 4. Parents have the main responsibility to protect their children online.
_____

☐ 5. Spending time in front of a computer screen is better than spending time in front of a television.
_____

☐ 6. Cellphone addiction is on the rise.
_____

☐ 7. The authors of a recent Nielsen study reported that online social networks are a key source of information and advice for many teens.
_____

☐ 8. Watching a movie in the movie theatre is a much better experience.
_____

☐ 9. Government censorship of the Internet improves Internet safety for young people.

☐ 10. Girls don't play video games.

☐ 11. Forty-five percent of teens globally say that they listen to five or more hours of music per week on their computer.

☐ 12. Online communities give people friends without responsibilities and commitments.

Exercise C
Write a topic sentence for each of the following topics.

1. trends in celebrity worship

2. independent music and big business

3. attraction of blogging

4. generational differences in cellphone use

5. Internet and reading skills

Exercise D
In each outline, cross out the sentences that don't support the topic sentence. Then write sentences that do support the topic sentence.

Outline 1
Topic Sentence: Too much leisure time for youth can get them into trouble.

— Supporting Sentence: Spend too much money
   { Supporting sentence: Youth should get part-time jobs to earn some money.
     Supporting sentence: Spend time hanging out at shopping malls. This tempts them to spend more money than they have.

— Supporting Sentence: Don't stay healthy
   { Supporting sentence: They don't have money to buy things, but they have enough money to eat fast food. They eat the wrong foods and can become fat.
     Supporting sentence: Spend time in front of the TV or computer screen. They don't get physical exercise; they also don't get enough sleep which can make them depressed.

— Supporting Sentence: Don't do well in school.
   { Supporting sentence: Become lazy and don't want to study hard in school
     Supporting sentence: If they don't do well in school, they will not get a job.

— Concluding sentence: Youth don't spend their leisure time productively. They should do more sports, play music, and read books.

Outline 2

Topic Sentence: Television networks produce reality TV shows because they're cheaper to make than traditional TV shows.

- Supporting Sentence: Don't need to pay much for actors.
  - Supporting sentence: Contestants are not professional actors. They want fame, not money.
  - Supporting sentence: Emotions of contestants are more natural than emotions of professional actors.
- Supporting Sentence: Don't need to hire professional writers to write a script.
  - Supporting sentence: Writers must write many drafts before they have a final script; takes time; professional writers are expensive.
  - Supporting sentence: What the actors say is a result of the situations they are in rather than a carefully written script.
- Supporting Sentence: Don't need to build an expensive set.
  - Supporting sentence: Programs are supposed to show real life, so sets don't need to be beautiful or extravagant.
  - Supporting sentence: More interesting to film in a real-life location.
- Concluding sentence: Reality TV shows are common because networks earn more money from them than from traditional programs.

Exercise E

Write a paragraph for one of the outlines in Exercise D.

☑ Persuasive Paragraph Checklist

Content
- ☐ Does my topic sentence state what my paragraph is about?
- ☐ Does my topic sentence clearly say what my perspective/attitude towards the topic (controlling idea) is?
- ☐ Is it clear that my purpose is to convince the reader that my perspective/attitude toward the topic is the truth?
- ☐ Will the ideas and information I have given (facts or statistics, expert opinion, examples, common sense) convince the reader to agree with my perspective/attitude toward the topic?
- ☐ Do all my statements connect to my perspective on the topic?
- ☐ Does my concluding sentence draw the reader's attention to the topic sentence again?

Organization
- ☐ Is the information in the paragraph organized in order of importance or in order of familiarity?
- ☐ Have I used words or phrases that show how the ideas are ordered (*first*, *the most important* [noun], *one* [noun], etc.)?

Meaning
- ☐ Have I used words properly to show the relationship between sentences (*therefore*, *however*, etc.)?
- ☐ Have I used precise words to communicate my meaning?

Mechanics
- ☐ Have I checked my paragraph for mistakes in grammar, spelling, and punctuation?

Exercise F

Make an outline for one of the topics in Exercises A, B, or C. Then write a paragraph from your outline.

Academic Word List

access	percent	technology
communicate	role	traditional
data	survey	
overall	task	

Word Meaning
Exercise A

Match each definition in Column A with the appropriate sample sentence in Column B.

Column A	Column B
1. a specific and often difficult job that someone has to do	a) Today many coffee shops give free **access** to the Internet.
2. set of questions that investigates a group of people's opinions or behaviours	b) Texting is the preferred way to **communicate** for youth.
3. based on beliefs, opinions or customs etc. that have been followed for a long time	c) The research **data** were collected in 42 countries around the world.
4. one part in every hundred	d) **Overall**, the media habits of teens are similar to the media habits of other age groups.
5. the application of scientific knowledge in industry	e) According to a recent online **survey** of adults and children in more than 12 countries, Canadian kids are least likely to have their parents in their cellphone address book.
6. express ideas or share information with others	
7. facts or information, often used to make decisions	f) Seventy **percent** of adults worldwide say that the Internet has made their relationships better.
8. a purpose that someone or something has in a situation or relationship	g) Our first **task** is to write the research questions.
9. the opportunity or right "to use" or "look at" something	h) The media play a major **role** in influencing people's opinions of political candidates.
10. when everything is considered	

i) Most youth want computers based on the latest **technology**.

j) The **traditional** approach to marketing included print ads and television.

Pronunciation
Exercise B

Listen to your teacher or an audio dictionary to hear the pronunciation of each word in the list. Repeat each word aloud. Mark the syllables and major word stress.

1. access (n)   àc / cess
2. communicate (v) _____
3. data (n pl) _____
4. overall (adv) _____
5. percent (n) _____
6. role (n) _____
7. survey (n) _____
8. task (n) _____
9. technology (n) _____
10. traditional (adj) _____

Word Forms
Exercise C

Fill in each blank with the word form shown in parentheses. Select only word forms that have the same meaning as in Exercise A.

1. access (n) _____ (v)
   _____ (adj)
   _____ (n)
2. communicate (v) _____ (adj)
   _____ (n)
   _____ (n)
3. data (n pl)
4. overall (adv) _____ (adj)
5. percent (n) _____ (n)

6. role (n)

7. survey (n) _____ (v)

8. task (n)

9. technology (n) _____ (adj)
   _____ (adv)
   _____ (n)

10. traditional (adj) _____ (adv)
    _____ (n)

Exercise D

In a dictionary, find one example sentence for each word in Exercise A and copy it into your notebook. Write a second sentence of your own. Then work with a partner to revise and edit your sentences.

Vocabulary in Context
Exercise E

Read the following paragraph and complete each blank with one of the words from the list. Use each word only once.

access	percentage	technology
communication	role	traditionally
data	surveyed	
overall	task	

When my family moved to Canada in the 1960s, talking to my grandparents back home in Germany was a big deal. ₁_____, people used the telephone to speak to family and friends who lived far away. Phone calls were expensive and the connection was not always good. My grandparents didn't even own a telephone at that time, but they had ₂_____ to a phone at a neighbour's apartment. So we called the neighbour, who ran next door, rang the bell to my grandparent's apartment and told them there was a call from Canada. My grandparents rushed to the telephone out of breath, anxious, and the calls were always short. The ₃_____ was simple. The phone had wires, a receiver, a round dial pad, and it rang. There were no push buttons, no call waiting, no hold, and no conference calls. ₄_____, the telephone didn't play a major ₅_____ in overseas ₆_____ back then. The ₇_____ of people phoning family overseas was small compared to today. Writing letters was much more common. Today's communication devices are much more sophisticated. Smart phones store ₈_____, games, movies, music, take photos, and connect to the Web. And "talking" has changed too. When a large communications company ₉_____ telephone subscribers a few years ago, they discovered that texting is the most popular method of communicating with loved ones overseas. It's quick and cheap. The ₁₀_____ for today's companies is to improve and add new features so that consumers stay interested and buy more. Today, calling family and friends around the world is a piece of cake.

Unit 5
Buyer Beware!

Vocabulary

Exercise A

Complete the following sentences by filling in the blanks with appropriate words from the vocabulary list below.

discount	sales pitch	recall	return policy
deal	consumer	promotions	contract
warranty	receipt	wholesale /	refund
knock-offs	store credit	retail	
counterfeit	scam	telemarketer	

1. The store clerk made an effective _____. I only intended to buy one item, but after she talked, I ended up buying five items.

2. They are opening up a number of new _____ stores on the first floor of the office tower. I'm looking forward to getting bargains.

3. I wanted to get a good deal on a new cellphone plan so I had to sign a _____. According to the agreement, I will pay $30 a month for the next three years.

4. It's a good thing I kept the _____. Since the pants didn't fit when I tried them on at home, I took the pants back to the store to get my money back.

5. I got the most amazing _____ on this kitchen appliance. I got this $300 machine on sale for $150.

6. Every year after the awards shows, manufacturers create _____ of the beautiful gowns that the stars were wearing. The gowns are much cheaper and look very similar to the really expensive designer gowns.

7. Since we are a charity, we asked the store to give us a substantial _____. We can't afford to pay the full retail price for things.

8. Always check the return policy before you purchase an item. This store does not return your money if you return an item. It only provides a _____ that you can use at their location in the future.

9. Unless a store has a "store credit only" return policy, you usually get the _____ in the same manner that you paid.

10. I'm really glad that I purchased the extended _____ on my new iPad. It broke after six months and I had to get it repaired.

The $2500 Pyramid

Exercise B

Each block of the pyramid below contains a list of words or phrases which relate to a vocabulary word from Exercise A. Award yourself the dollar amount for each word you guess correctly. For each of your answers, write a sentence demonstrating your understanding of the word.

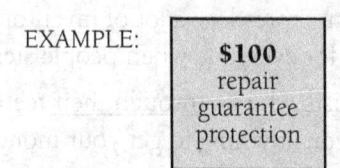

EXAMPLE:

$100
repair
guarantee
protection

Answer: Things that relate to "warranty"

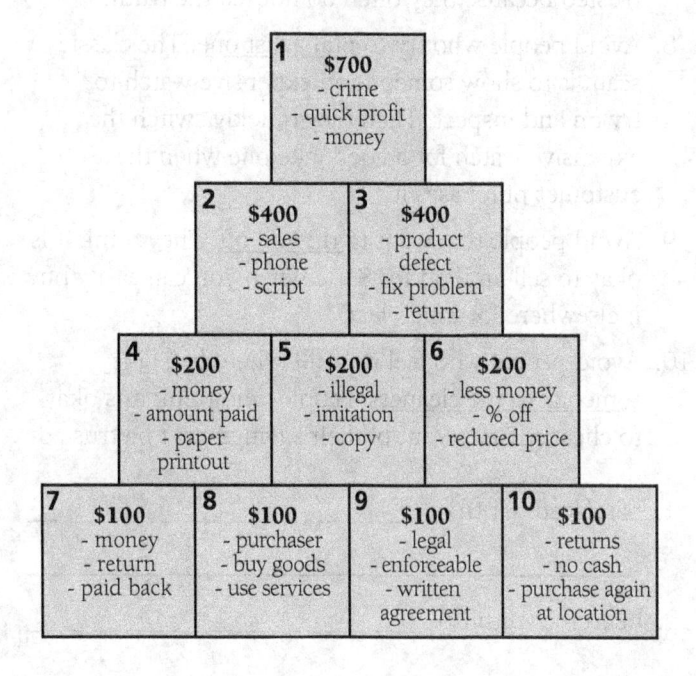

1. $700
   - crime
   - quick profit
   - money

2. $400
   - sales
   - phone
   - script

3. $400
   - product defect
   - fix problem
   - return

4. $200
   - money
   - amount paid
   - paper printout

5. $200
   - illegal
   - imitation
   - copy

6. $200
   - less money
   - % off
   - reduced price

7. $100
   - money
   - return
   - paid back

8. $100
   - purchaser
   - buy goods
   - use services

9. $100
   - legal
   - enforceable
   - written agreement

10. $100
    - returns
    - no cash
    - purchase again at location

Vocabulary Expansion

Exercise C

Read "Ten Tips for Avoiding Dishonest People." Try to determine the meaning of the underlined idioms. Write a brief definition for each idiom.

Ten Tips for Avoiding Dishonest People

1. Avoid <u>barefaced liars</u> who can look you in the eye and easily tell you a complete falsehood without feeling any shame.
2. Avoid people who regularly <u>bend the truth</u>. They might tell you that they have completed the project when in fact they haven't finished the final steps.
3. Avoid people who are selling products on the <u>black market</u>. When you buy illegal products, you are breaking the law.
4. Avoid people who have been <u>caught red-handed</u>. Associating with people who have been caught doing criminal activities is bad for your reputation.
5. Avoid people who think that a <u>five-finger discount</u> is an acceptable way to get goods without paying any money for them. Stores lose a lot of inventory and the price increases for everyone when people steal.
6. Avoid scam artists who <u>lie through their teeth</u>. They will easily tell you anything to get your money.
7. Avoid people who tell a <u>pack of lies</u>. They can't be trusted because they often do not tell the truth.
8. Avoid people who try to <u>pull a fast one</u>. The classic scam is to show someone an expensive watch to try on and inspect. Then they quickly switch the expensive watch for a good fake one when the customer purchases it.
9. Avoid people that want to <u>rip you off</u>. They think it is okay to sell an iPod for $300 when you can easily buy it elsewhere for much less.
10. Avoid people who feel no guilt when they <u>take someone to the cleaners</u>. People who think it is okay to cheat someone out of their savings can't be trusted.

1. barefaced liar (n) _____
2. bend the truth (v) _____
3. black market (n) _____
4. catch someone red-handed (v) _____
5. five-finger discount (n) _____
6. lie through your teeth (v) _____
7. pack of lies (n) _____
8. pull a fast one (v) _____
9. rip you off (v) _____
10. take to the cleaners (v) _____

Exercise D

List the idioms in Exercise C beside the appropriate headings.

lie: _____

cheat: _____

steal: _____

Exercise E

Complete the following sentences with one of the following idiomatic expressions.

barefaced liar	lying through my teeth
bending the truth	pack of lies
bent the truth	pulled a fast one
black market	ripped me off
caught the kid red-handed	ripped off
five-finger discount	taken to the cleaners

1. It is really hard to believe John. He told me that he had a Ph.D. and a really good job that paid him the big bucks. He also said that his girlfriend was a

gorgeous supermodel and they lived in a million-dollar condo downtown. I just found out he is broke and lives with his parents. Everything he said was a _____.

2. It's hard to be a teenager with little spending money, but getting something by a _____ is not a good idea. Taking the item you really want without paying for it can give you a criminal record for the rest of your life.

3. I made a bad investment and got _____. My financial advisor gave me wrong information about an investment. I lost almost all my money when the value of the property dropped by 90 percent.

4. I _____ a little when I told my husband I got a really good discount on that expensive purse. I really only got 10 percent off, but I know he doesn't like it when I spend a lot of money on accessories.

5. There is a thriving _____ in counterfeit purses. You can buy an almost exact replica of a $2000 bag for $100.

6. I think that shopkeeper _____. I'm sure the earrings I purchased had three red stones and these ones only have two. I think he switched them when he was wrapping them up.

7. That shopkeeper _____. He charged me $35 for that item even though the tag on the shelf said it cost $25.

8. My boss is a _____. He told all of us employees that the store was losing money, so he couldn't give us a raise. Then we found out that the store made $300,000 profit last year.

9. I don't like working as a commissioned sales person. I often end up _____ to try and convince a customer to buy something. I always feel bad afterwards when I think about all the exaggerated claims I made to get a sale.

10. The security camera _____ when he put the CD in his pocket and walked out of the store without paying for it.

Grammar Focus

Gerunds
Exercise A
Complete the sentences with a gerund form of one of the verbs from the box. Use each word only once.

learn	tell	work	shop
smoke	drive	make	
get	eat	find	

1. _____ is becoming more and more expensive as the price of gas goes up.

2. _____ 40+ hours a week is tiring, but I need the money.

3. _____ at expensive restaurants is a truly enjoyable experience.

4. _____ about popular scams makes you an informed consumer.

5. _____ a raise means I can afford to move out of my parents' house.

6. _____ a good buy makes me happy.

7. _____ a lie to your partner is not a good idea.

8. _____ is one of my favourite things to do when I have some free time.

Exercise B
Write sentences to describe the following subjects. Use a gerund in each sentence.

Example: best vacation: visit
           My best vacation was visiting Niagara Falls.

1. most interesting sport: box _____
   _____

2. favourite activity: read _____
   _____

3. convince people purchase knock-off: easy _____
   _____

4. idea of a good time: _____
   _____

5. purchase TV: thrill _____
   _____

6. find bargain: excite _____
   _____

7. get ripped off: aggravate _____
   _____

8. catch thief: reward _____
   _____

Exercise C
Read about the arrest in the Nigerian email scan. Complete the sentences using information from the story.

The RCMP arrested three men yesterday after a year-long investigation into the Nigerian email scam. The police were able to identify more than 300 victims. This scam has been around for more than a decade, but people continue to fall for it. These scam artists got the contact information for potential victims from professional associations and corporate directories. They then sent out thousands of emails to request help. The email typically asked for help to transfer money out of Nigeria into financial institutions in the victim's country. The letter asked for the person to pay the expenses to transfer the millions to the victim's account. The amount seemed small when they were promised millions if they helped move the money. If the victim agreed, they first sent small amounts and then the con artists asked for more and more money. Some of the victims lost anywhere from $50,000 to more than $5 million.

1. The RCMP delayed _____ the men until they had completed their year-long investigation.

2. They report _____ more than 300 victims.

3. Even though the scam is well-known, people keep _____ for it.

4. The con artists preferred _____ professional people that they identified in professional associations and corporate directories.

5. The scammer asked the potential victims for help _____ money out of Nigeria into a bank in the victim's country.

6. If the victim started _____ small amounts of money, they were asked for more.

7. The con artists continued _____ the victim to send more and more money.

8. Some victims reported _____ anywhere from $50,000 to more than $5 million.

Exercise D
Complete each of the following sentences using a gerund.

1. You need to be careful to avoid _____ ripped off when purchasing a major item.

2. The con artist couldn't deny _____ people when questioned by the police.

3. I suggest _____ the bill carefully before exiting the store.

4. She can't help not _____ him because he always lies.

5. They dislike _____ the full price for anything. They only want to purchase items when they are on sale.

6. Do you appreciate _____ the details or would you rather read it for yourself?

7. I want to discuss _____ a warranty with you first before the sales person tries to talk me into spending the extra money.

8. You risk _____ scammed if you purchase something through a phone sales call.

Exercise E
Join the following pairs of sentences by beginning each new sentence with the words in italics.

EXAMPLE: Someone needs to watch out for shoplifters.
Security guards are appropriate for this.
Security guards are appropriate for watching out for shoplifters.

1. It is hard to identify counterfeit purses because they look so real. *Janice is concerned about* that.
   _____

2. Mike can easily determine if someone is lying. *Mike is good at* that.
   _____

3. He shops every day after work. *He is tired of* that.
   _____

4. I try not to get ripped off. *I'm afraid of* this.
   _____

5. She doesn't want to get caught stealing. *She is worried about* that.
_____

6. I'm wondering if I can use the video tape to identify the thief. *The video tape should be suitable for* that.
_____

7. Kim planned to take a great trip. *Kim was excited about* it.
_____

8. Hakim keeps track of the number of goods stolen each week. *Hakim is responsible for* that.
_____

Exercise F
Complete the sentences with the appropriate preposition from the box (use more than once) and the gerund form of the verb in parentheses.

| at | on | in | to | about | for | of | by |

1. Li is extremely excited _____ (buy) her first car.
2. Larry was surprised _____ (find) the kitchen appliance on sale for half price.
3. I always insist _____ (check) the item over carefully before I purchase it.
4. He is angry _____ (get) ripped off at that store.
5. He isn't concerned _____ (have) enough money for the stereo.
6. She is overwhelmed _____ (have) so many job responsibilities.
7. I believe _____ (do) the right thing if possible.
8. She is accused _____ (steal) an MP3 player.
9. Do you have a reason _____ (lie) all the time?
10. I look forward _____ (visit) that new mall.

Grammar Edit
The fraud squad has written the following warning to post on their website. However, before it can be posted, someone needs to correct the 12 errors in gerund usage.

Cross out the mistakes and write the correct form above each.

Consumers should watch out for the following scams that make them think they can earn a lot of money quickly.

1. **Stuffing Envelopes at Home** (2 errors)

   For a small fee a company promises to show you how to earn money while working at home. Avoid get scammed. All you get for your money is a letter telling you to place similar ads (at your expense) to recruit others. If you do this, you are responsible for scam other innocent people.

2. **Assembly or Craft Work at Home** (4 errors)

   The ads propose make lots of money for goods you either make or put together at home. The person you contact strongly advises buy expensive materials and equipment from the company first that are necessary to get started. Then the company never ends up purchase the items you have made. You never get your investment money back or earn any extra. Pay for the necessary materials is a scam.

3. **Computer Work at Home** (2 errors)

   A company claims you can earn money doing data entry and word processing from home. After you contact the company, it insists on receive a small fee for the initial set-up. People report get a useless guide with only a few business contacts in companies that are not legitimate or pay very little.

4. **Pyramid Schemes** (2 errors)

You get excited about make big money selling products. You earn commissions on your own sales. The company also strongly recommends recruit others, so you can earn commissions from their sales as well. Only the people at the top (those that began this distribution chain) make any real money.

(2 errors)

Don't risk lose your money. Get scammed is frustrating. Legitimate companies don't require fees to get further information or try to pressure you to make a fast decision. If you come across one of these ads offering to give you big money for little effort or the opportunity to get rich quick, ignore it. Chances are it is just another version of these popular successful scams.

Reading

Guided Summary

Ways Stores Get You to Spend More Than You Think

A summary is a short, concise piece of writing that requires you to put the main points of the reading in your own words. It is always shorter than the original reading.

Write a summary of "Ways Stores Get You to Spend More Than You Think" on pages 60–61 in the Student Book. Write point-form notes to answer the questions. Use the information to write your summary.

1. What is the main idea of the reading?
2. Explain the following:

   Double Discount
   What is it? _____
   _____
   What common mistake do consumers make?
   _____
   _____

   Buy One, Get One Free
   What is it? _____
   _____
   What common mistake do consumers make?
   _____

   "Sale" Doesn't Mean a Discount Price
   What is it? _____
   _____
   What common mistake do consumers make?
   _____

Phone Scams to Get Your Money

Write a summary of "Phone Scams to Get Your Money," on page 62 in the Student Book. Write point-form notes to answer the questions. Use the information to write your summary.

1. What is the main idea of the reading?
2. Describe the following phone scams:

The Sweepstakes Pitch: _____
_____
_____

Emergency or "Grandparent" Scam: _____
_____
_____

Writing

Model Paragraph

There are several ways that con artists persuade people to give away their money. <u>For one thing</u>, they lie, cheat, and trick people. In one popular scam, <u>for example</u>, people are promised a lot of money if
5 they help to get a large amount of money out of a country such as Nigeria. The scammers ask people to send some of their own money first to pay for the transfer tax or processing fee. The scammers promise that 10 times that amount will be given back to the
10 person once the money is moved out of the country.

The victims never receive any money back. A second way con artists trick their victims is by studying the character of potential victims and then appealing to their greed, loneliness, insecurity, poor health,
15 or ignorance. They know that most people want to make a lot of money, and this makes people like any idea that promises to make them a lot of money. People often make bad decisions when their desire to make money is stronger than their desire to think
20 intelligently. In addition, con artists use their charm to make victims trust them and then persuade their victims to give them money. Con artists are not easy to spot. They do not look suspicious. Actually, their appearance is one way they gain their victim's trust.
25 If they are trying to cheat possible rich investors, they will wear expensive suits and flash around a lot of money. When they target seniors in a home-improvement scam, they will show up in work clothes and behave like an experienced contractor.
30 Finally, con artists carefully watch how their scams are working, so they know when the con is no longer workable. They move on to another location after they have taken many people to the cleaners and before the police catch them. Con artists have a lot of confidence
35 in their ability to gain people's trust and they have several ways to carry out their scams.

1. What is the writer's aim in this paragraph?
2. What is the topic of this paragraph? Underline the sentence that tells what this paragraph is about.
3. What kind of evidence is given to support the point of view stated in the topic sentence: research, examples, comparisons, stories?

Expository Paragraphs
The expository paragraph is written to explain something to the reader. It provides explanations that convincingly illustrate the main point: research, examples, comparisons, and stories.

Exercise A

For each of the topic sentences, write out the topic and the key idea that will be explained. You can review topic sentences on page 135 in the Appendix.

EXAMPLE: Victor Lustig was one of the most confident tricksters that ever lived.

  Topic: Lustig was a trickster
  Controlling idea: most confident

1. Items marked "sale" are not always being sold for a special price.
   Topic: _____
   Controlling idea: _____
2. One of the greatest swindlers in American history was Victor Ponzi.
   Topic: _____
   Controlling idea: _____
3. When I was growing up, one of the activities I enjoyed most was going to garage sales with my mom.
   Topic: _____
   Controlling idea: _____
4. It is a fact that con artists feel no remorse for taking people's money.
   Topic: _____
   Controlling idea: _____
5. Being a careful consumer is the key to not getting ripped off.
   Topic: _____
   Controlling idea: _____

Exercise B

Identify the functions of the following sentences. Write the correct number on the line.

1. Topic sentence
2. General supporting point for the topic sentence
3. Example to illustrate the supporting point

4. Commentary that explains how the example supports the topic sentence
5. Concluding sentence / restatement of topic sentence

___5___ a) Going to garage sales during the summer can be a lot of fun and who knows—you may even get the buy of a lifetime.

_____ b) Occasionally, people sell valuable items that they think are worthless.

_____ c) My aunt picked up a vase for fifty cents that she sold to a collector for $500.

_____ d) Last year I purchased a new $50 marble cheese tray with pewter handles and cheese knives still in the box for $3.

_____ e) Getting great bargains like these makes going to garage sales worthwhile.

_____ f) People sell both new and used items cheap just to get rid of them.

_____ g) If you are knowledgeable about art or antiques you may be able to scoop up a valuable find for next to nothing.

_____ h) I heard about one man who bought a painting for fifty bucks that turned out to be a painting by someone famous worth millions.

_____ i) The best place to find a great bargain is at a garage sale.

_____ j) I picked up several bestsellers for $1 each.

Exercise C

The preceding sentences are out of order. Write the sentences in the correct order to complete the outline.

Topic Sentence: _____

_____

General Point 1 (Reason): _____

_____

Example for Point 1: _____

_____

Example for Point 1: _____

_____

Commentary on Point 1: _____

_____

General Point 2 (Reason): _____

_____

Example for Point 2: _____

_____

Example for Point 2: _____

_____

Commentary on Point 2: _____

_____

Concluding Sentence: _____

_____

Exercise D

Everything in the paragraph must relate to the controlling idea in the topic sentence to create a sense of unity. All general points must relate to the topic sentence. Examples and other details must illustrate the general point. Any sentence that does not relate to the key idea in the topic sentence is irrelevant and does not belong in the paragraph. Cross out any sentences that do not support the general points listed below.

1. Items marked "sale" are not always being sold for a special price.
   a) The cereal displayed at the end of the aisle with a sale sign is the same price it is every week.
   b) I always buy it because it is my favourite cereal.
   c) People should always check their grocery flyer for sales.
   d) The detergent cost $3 last week. This week it is advertised in the sales flyer for $3.

2. One of the greatest swindlers in American history was Victor Ponzi.
   a) In 1920, he was living in the United States.
   b) He bought discounted coupons in one country and sold them for face value in the United States.
   c) He made millions with his pyramid money scheme.
   d) After leaving jail he worked occasionally as a translator.

3. When I was growing up, one of the activities I enjoyed most was going to garage sales with my mom.
   a) We always went at 6:00 a.m.

b) Spending Saturday mornings shopping for treasures was fun.
c) Mom and I loved to pick up cheap books that people often sold for a buck.
d) The garage sales were in our neighbourhood.

Exercise E

Write a sentence that explains how the examples in Exercise D support the general points.

1. _____
2. _____
3. _____

Exercise F

Underline the words or phrases the writer uses in order to write a coherent paragraph.

1. Con artists often target the elderly. For instance, fake contractors try to talk them into paying for unnecessary repairs to their homes.
2. People think that if it is on the end shelf, it is on sale. Moreover, they think it is on sale for a significant discount.
3. The seller didn't know the true value of the antique. Consequently, I got it at a really cheap price.
4. It was marked down 50 percent. As a result, it sold out quickly.
5. I got a great bargain. I bought a kitchen appliance 40 percent off, for example.
6. First of all, sale items are moved to a special section. Second, they are marked down with red stickers.
7. I bought this chair there. I also got this lamp.
8. I only purchase something I really need. Furthermore, I refuse to use credit cards.

Exercise G

Add connecting words to the sentences in Exercise B to create a coherent paragraph.

Exercise H

Expository paragraphs are used to explain something. Write a paragraph about one of the following topics:
- how con artists scam elderly people
- how the Net Generation shops
- how marketing can influence your purchases

✔ Expository Paragraph Checklist

Content
☐ Does my topic sentence indicate what the paragraph will explain?
☐ Does my topic sentence clearly say what my perspective or attitude toward the topic is?
☐ Have I used clear, meaningful examples to illustrate the general points?
☐ Does my concluding sentence draw the reader's attention to the topic sentence again?

Organization
☐ Is the information in the paragraph organized in order of importance, order of familiarity, or time order?

Meaning
☐ Have I used words appropriately to show the relationships between sentences?
☐ Have I used precise words to communicate my meaning?

Mechanics
☐ Have I checked my paragraph for mistakes in grammar, spelling, and punctuation?

Academic Word List

assume	item	specifically	transfer
contact	purchase	strategies	
individual	register	target	

Word Meaning
Exercise A
Circle the word that best matches the meaning

1. the movement of something from one place to another (purchase, transfer, assume)
2. begin communication with (contact, purchase, target)
3. a single human being (target, contact, individual)
4. buy (purchase, transfer, assume)
5. put name on a formal list* (register, purchase, assume)
6. particularly (individual, specifically, strategies)
7. article (individual, item, target)
8. to focus on a particular group of people (target, contact, transfer)
9. plans (target, transfer, strategies)
10. accept as being true even before knowing it for certain (assume, specifically, target)

*the meaning is different from the meaning in the reading, but the verb form is the most popular usage of this word.

Pronunciation
Exercise B
Listen to your teacher or an audio dictionary to hear the pronunciation of each word in the list. Repeat each word aloud. Mark the syllables and major word stress.

1. assume (v)   as / **sùme**
2. contacts (v)   _____
3. individual (n)   _____
4. item (n)   _____
5. purchase (v)   _____
6. register (v)   _____
7. specifically (adv) _____
8. strategies (n)   _____
9. targets (v)   _____
10. transfer (n)   _____

Word Forms
Exercise C
Fill in each blank with the word form shown in parentheses. Select only word forms that have the same meaning as in Exercise A.

1. assume (v): _____ (n)
   _____ (adj)
2. contact (v): _____ (n)
3. individual (n): _____ (adj)
   _____ (v)
   _____ (adv)
   _____ (n)
4. item (n): _____ (v)
5. purchase (v): _____ (n)
   _____ (adj)
   _____ (n)
6. register (v): _____ (n)
7. specifically (adv): _____ (adj)
   _____ (n)
8. strategies (n): _____ (v)
   _____ (adj)
   _____ (adv)
   _____ (n)
9. targets (v): _____ (n)
10. transfer (n): _____ (adj)
    _____ (n)
    _____ (v)

Exercise D
In a dictionary, find one example sentence for each word in Exercise A and copy it into your notebook. Write a second sentence of your own. Then, work with a partner to revise and edit your sentences.

Vocabulary in Context
Exercise E
Read the following paragraph and complete each blank with one of the words from the list. Use each word only once.

assumed	purchased	targeted
contacted	registered	transfer
individual	specifically	
item	strategy	

Victor Lustig was one of the most talented con artists in history. Born in 1890, he was an extremely charming 1_____ who could speak many languages. One of his first scams involved a money printing machine. He 2_____ passengers travelling on the ocean liner between Paris and New York City. He showed clients that a small box printed a $100 bill, but he said it took six hours to do so. Thinking they could get rich, clients 3_____ the box for up to $30,000. In the next 12 hours, the box printed two more $100 bills and then only blank pieces of paper after that. Lustig left and disappeared before the clients realized they had been cheated.

In 1925, Lustig read a newspaper article that said the city was having trouble maintaining the Eiffel Tower. This gave him an idea. He said he was a government official and people just 4_____ that was true. He 5_____ six different scrap metal dealers and invited them to discuss a business deal. He told them that the upkeep of the Eiffel Tower was expensive and that it was an 6_____ that the city could no longer afford to maintain. He told them the city 7_____ wanted to 8_____ ownership of the tower to a dealer, so it could be used for scrap metal. He sold the tower to one dealer and took a train to Vienna with the dealer's money. Lustig's outrageous 9_____ was successful. The scrap dealer discovered that Lustig had never 10_____ him as owner of the Eiffel Tower on any official government documents. The dealer was so embarrassed when he found out he had been conned that he never went to the police.

Lustig eventually got arrested in the United States for counterfeiting. He died in Alcatraz of pneumonia, but he will go down in history as the man who sold the Eiffel Tower.

Unit 6
Catch Me If You Can

Vocabulary

Exercise A

Match the verb in Column A with its definition in Column B.

Column A	Column B
1. accuse	a) to take something from a person or store without permission or paying for it
2. arrest	b) to kill somebody deliberately
3. assault	c) to be searched for by the police in connection with a crime
4. be wanted	d) to take and hold someone at a police station because the police believe the person may be guilty of a crime
5. book someone	e) to decide and state officially in court that somebody is guilty of a crime
6. break into	f) to say that somebody has done something wrong or is guilty of something
7. convict	g) to enter a building by force
8. investigate	h) to carefully examine the facts of a situation, an event, or a crime to find out the truth about it or how it happened
9. steal	i) to attack somebody physically
10. murder	j) for law enforcement to write down somebody's name and address because they have committed a crime or an offence

Exercise B

Use a form of the verbs from Exercise A to complete the following sentences.

1. He _____ the woman when he punched her in the face.
2. Someone _____ our house on the weekend and stole all of our electronic equipment.
3. The police _____ the break-in and trying to find the thief.
4. I _____ my roommate of taking $20 from my wallet while I was sleeping.
5. The court _____ the accused man because of the evidence against him.
6. She _____ makeup and ran from the store.
7. The police _____ the girl for shoplifting.
8. If you _____ someone, you will go to jail for 20 years to life.
9. The police arrested the woman, took her to the station and _____ for shoplifting.
10. He _____ by the police for stealing a car.

Exercise C

The clues define people associated with a crime. Use the clues to complete the crossword.

attacker	investigators	the accused
criminal	paramedic	thief
detective	police officer	
eyewitness	suspect	

Down:

1. people who examine a situation such as an accident or a crime to find out the truth
2. a person whose job is to examine crimes and catch criminals
3. a person who wears a uniform and whose job is to make people obey the law
4. a person who steals from a person or place, especially using violence or threats
5. a person who the police believe has committed a crime
9. a person connected with or involved in a crime

Across:

6. the person who is on trial for committing a crime
7. a person who has seen a crime or accident and can describe it afterwards
8. a person who acts with violence towards somebody to hurt them
10. a person whose job is to help people who are sick or injured, but who is not a doctor or a nurse

Exercise D

Use a word from the list to complete each sentence.

abduction	fingerprints	theft
alibi	forensic evidence	vandalism
arson	photographs	victim
firearms	shoplifting	

1. Police charged the teens with _____. They got caught spray painting words on the side of the school.
2. It is illegal to carry _____ in Canada. In the United States, however, people can carry guns with them to many places. Can you imagine taking a weapon with you to the supermarket when you go shopping?
3. They suspect that the cause of the fire was _____. The police found an empty gas can and a lighter in the bushes next to the house that burned.
4. Did you read about the _____ in the paper? A girl was taken from her room while everyone in the house was sleeping. The police are searching for the person who took her.
5. The _____ of the famous painting shocked everyone. The museum was supposed to be very secure and impossible to break into.
6. Police dusted the crime scene for _____. Each person has a distinct pattern of lines on the ends of their fingers. The investigators can match the prints at the crime scene to prints in their database. They will know who committed the crime.
7. The police have used the most advanced scientific techniques to gather detailed proof at the crime scene. They hope to use this _____ to convict the criminal.
8. The _____ that the police took will be used as evidence. These pictures are usually taken with a digital camera.
9. My friend got caught for _____. He put a watch in his backpack when the shopkeeper was busy with another customer and walked out of the store. The shopkeeper had a surveillance camera and recorded it all.
10. The person that the police thought robbed the bank had an _____ for where he was when the robbery occurred. Police talked to his boss and confirmed that he was in a meeting with his boss at that exact time.
11. The latest _____ was a 40-year-old woman. She was robbed at gunpoint and had all of her jewellery stolen.

Vocabulary Expansion

Phrasal Verbs
Exercise E

The prepositions *of*, *for*, *into*, and *from* commonly follow verbs. Write the crime verb under the appropriate preposition.

accuse (someone)	book (someone)	investigate
arrest (someone)	break	steal (something)
be wanted	convict	

of	for	into	from

Exercise F

Complete the sentences with an appropriate verb + preposition from Exercise E. Change the verb to the appropriate tense.

1. The police read the man his rights and _____ him _____ robbing the convenience store. Then, they put him in the police car and took him to jail.

2. When the police took the man to jail, they _____ him _____ robbing the convenience store. They took his fingerprints and all of his personal belongings and put him in a jail cell.

3. The security system and bars on the windows make it difficult for anyone to _____ _____ our house now.

4. The shopkeeper _____ the teen _____ shoplifting, but when the police searched the teen, they found no evidence.

5. Take a look at the police sketch of this man. He _____ _____ armed robbery. He is considered dangerous. The police are looking for him. If you see him, call the police.

6. The detectives are _____ the man _____ fraud. They think he cheated his investors, so now they are examining all his documents.

7. Someone _____ my car _____ the driveway during the night. Now I have no car.

8. The prosecutors had very convincing forensic evidence. As a result, the judge _____ the man _____ murder.

Grammar Focus

Passive Voice
Exercise A

Write the following sentences in the passive voice since the doer of the action is not important or not known. Remove the doer of the action from the sentence.

Example: They protect the crime scene with yellow tape.
The crime scene is protected with yellow tape.

1. They collect fingerprints at the crime scene.
   _____

2. They might identify the murderer soon.
   _____

3. They could find evidence at the scene.
   _____

4. They take lots of pictures of the scene.
   _____

5. They may identify the thief using trace evidence.
   _____

6. They use blood spatters to help determine what happened.
   _____

7. They collect insect evidence to help establish time of death.
   _____

8. They stole millions of dollars from the armoured truck.
   _____

Exercise B

Choose the word or phrase that best completes each sentence.

1. Fingerprints can _____ from a crime scene years later using high intensity laser lights.
   a) recover
   b) been recovered
   c) be recovered
   d) will be recovered

2. Every four hours the property _____ by security.
   a) checks
   b) was checking
   c) is checked
   d) will check

3. The police _____ the suspect two blocks from the scene last night.
   a) arrested
   b) will have arrested
   c) is arrested
   d) might be arrested

4. The police announced that a prime suspect _____.
   a) has been arrested
   b) is arrested
   c) will arrest
   d) arrested

5. The policed announced that a prime suspect _____ at 10:00 this morning.
   a) has been arrested
   b) is arrested
   c) will arrest
   d) was arrested

6. The police _____ as much evidence as possible before they release the crime scene.
   a) have gathered
   b) will gather
   c) be gathered
   d) will be gathered

7. Whenever someone _____ a surface, they leave behind trace evidence.
   a) has touched
   b) will have touched
   c) touches
   d) will touch

8. In the next step, the fingerprints _____ by the police.
   a) will be collected
   b) was collected
   c) can collect
   d) collected

Exercise C

Use the passive voice form of the verbs in parentheses to complete the story "The Amazing Trace Case." Include the agent only if necessary.

In 1923, a train ₁ <u>was robbed</u>.
(rob) (robber)

The train crew ₂ _____.
(murder) (robber)

The police investigated the crime. A pair of greasy overalls ₃ _____ at the
(find) (police)

scene. The overalls ₄ _____
(send) (clerk)

to Edward Heinrich, the boss at a forensics laboratory. Forensic evidence ₅ _____,
(find) (Heinrich)

allowing him to create a profile of the killer.

The profile ₆ _____ to
(deliver) (mailman)

the detectives. The detectives ₇ _____ to look for a
(inform) (letter)

tall, left-handed lumberjack with light brown hair, in his early 20s, weighing approximately 75 kilograms and living somewhere near the town of Hurndale.

Clues, such as the size of the overalls, hair caught in the button, tree-sap stains on the overalls, and a faded postal receipt from the pocket ₈ _____ to create such
(use) (Heinrich)

a precise description.

Residents of Hurndale ₉ _____.
(question) (police)

A man fitting the exact description ₁₀ _____.
(identify) (someone)

The police went to the man's house. He confessed to the murder and 11 _____ (arrest) (police). He thought he had gotten away with murder, but the trace evidence he had left behind helped to convict him in the end.

Exercise D

Which of the following sentences can be changed to passive voice? If the sentence cannot be changed, write *No change*.

Example: The thief didn't find the hidden safe.
The hidden safe wasn't found.

When did the robbery happen? *No change*

1. The thief took a valuable coin collection.
   _____
2. The coins were worth thousands of dollars.
   _____
3. They were commemorative gold coins.
   _____
4. The police dusted the entire room for fingerprints.
   _____
5. They found three partial fingerprints and one good print.
   _____
6. They ran the fingerprints through CODIS.
   _____
7. There was no match on the CODIS search.
   _____
8. Hopefully, other evidence will help police find the thief.
   _____

Grammar Edit

Read about the robbery reported in the local paper. Find and correct the three mistakes in tense and five mistakes in form related to the passive voice.

Late last night, an unknown intruder broke into the home of millionaire Jared Singh. Police say that the intruder broke in through a window at the back of the house that will be left open by mistake. Fingerprints were find on the windowsill and glass. Investigators used black powder to highlight the fingerprint patterns. Dozens of pictures were be taken as evidence. A boot print will also be found in one of the rooms. It indicates that the thief wears a size 11 shoe. A large quantity of cash and jewellery was take. Singh reported that a diamond ring that had been in his family for over three generations was missing. Also stolen, was a priceless painting by Degas that had hung in his study. Local pawn shops and art dealers have be notified to be on the lookout for the stolen goods. The police think that the robber will try to sell the items quickly. Singh will be questioned by the police for several hours. They wanted to know why his security system was not on last night. Singh reported that the security system had been turn on before he went out for the evening. Now the police suspect that the thief must have been someone who was familiar with the home and knew how to disable the security alarm.

Reading

Guided Summary

A summary is a short, concise piece of writing that requires you to put the main points of the reading in your own words. It is always shorter than the original reading.

The reading describes a crime scene and the investigative process used to process the scene. Use the questions on the next page as a guide to write a summary of the reading on pages 74–76 of the Student Book.

	The Crime	**The Investigation Process**
The Crime Scene	1. Where did the crime occur? 2. What did the police find at the crime scene?	1. What does the forensic team do at a crime scene?
Fingerprints	3. What fingerprints were collected and where were they located?	2. How are fingerprints collected? 3. How do fingerprints differ from each other? 4. How do investigators determine if there is a known match to the fingerprints?
Blood File	4. Where was blood found at the crime scene? 5. What do the police do to find and collect it?	5. How do the police find all the blood evidence? 6. How is the location of blood evidence recorded? 7. What do the police do with the blood? 8. How is the blood used to identify a person?
Insect Evidence	6. What other type of evidence do police collect at the scene? 7. What conclusions can they make about the murder based on the insect evidence?	9. What do the police do with eggs and maggots from a crime scene? 10. How do the police use information from insects in their investigation?

Writing

Model Paragraph

Fingerprints found at a crime scene are very important for the identification of the criminal. Technicians need to follow a specific process to ensure getting usable prints. First, the technician
5 needs to identify surfaces that might have fingerprints. Smooth surfaces such as glass and mirrors are good locations. Every person has perspiration and oil on their fingers. The unique patterns of ridges on our fingers transfer to surfaces that we touch. To get this
10 evidence, technicians pour a small amount of powder on a piece of paper. They use white powder for dark surfaces and black powder for light surfaces. Next, they dip the tip of a brush into the powder and gently tap the brush to remove any excess powder. Then,
15 using short quick strokes, they run the brush's bristles lightly over the surface where they think the prints are. The powder sticks to the oily ridges and reveals the fingerprints. Once the prints are revealed, the next step is to lift the prints. To do this, the technicians
20 gently press cellophane tape on top of the print. Then, with one quick motion, they pull the clear tape away from the surface. The final step involves attaching the tape with the print to a piece of paper. This method of collecting fingerprints has been used by crime-scene
25 investigators for many years.

1. What is the writer's aim in this paragraph?
2. What process is being described?
3. How is the information organized?
4. What words are used to show the order of the process?
5. What words are used to show how things are done?

Process Paragraphs

A process paragraph is a step-by-step explanation or description that tells the reader how to complete a task or how something works. The purpose of the paragraph is stated at the beginning, and then the steps are explained in chronological order. The imperative mood and the passive voice are commonly used in process paragraphs.

Process paragraphs use listing signals (*first, second, next, then, third, last, finally*) to make the order of events clear. The listing signals (*the first, the second, the next, the third, the last, the final*) are used with process enumerators (*first step, the first stage, in the first phase*).

Exercise A

The topic sentence in a process paragraph introduces the topic and tells the reader how the information will be organized. Identify the best topic sentence for a process paragraph about:

1. dusting for fingerprints
   a) This is how you dust for fingerprints.
   b) Dusting for fingerprints is not that difficult once you have learned these few steps.
   c) Follow these five instructions.

2. protecting your home from burglary
   a) Burglars should not be able to break into your home.
   b) It's upsetting when your house is broken into.
   c) Following five simple guidelines will help keep burglars out of your home.

3. how a home alarm works
   a) Understanding how your home alarm works will help you protect your home.
   b) Home alarms are effective for protecting your home.
   c) Many people have home alarm systems.

4. Securing a crime scene …
   a) is a straightforward, five-step process.
   b) is the first step when investigating a crime scene.
   c) is important when you investigate a crime scene.

5. Protecting yourself from identity theft …
   a) is quite easy if you are careful.
   b) is very difficult, but possible.
   c) is possible if you carefully follow these four good practices.

6. Telephone scammers …
   a) follow predictable steps to get your money.
   b) try to gain your confidence to get your money.
   c) target the elderly.

Exercise B

The imperative mood is usually used to give a strong and direct instruction. It allows us to avoid using "you" too often. First, put the words in order to make a sentence. Then make imperative sentences by crossing out any unnecessary words.

Example: doors ~~You~~ deadbolts on install all exterior ~~should~~.

~~You should~~ *Install deadbolts on all exterior doors.*

1. windows You lock should all.
   _____

2. you the outside house should install sensitive lights motion around of your I think.
   _____

3. garage You the put all must ladders in
   _____

4. basement I you on bars the advise windows put to.
   _____

5. mail You also to delivery all of papers are advised and stop.
   _____

Exercise C

The passive voice can also be used to show that an action is done without saying who does the action. Change the following sentences to the passive voice. Eliminate the doer of the action.

Example: Someone scans the fingerprints to create a digital file.

The fingerprints are scanned to create a digital file.

1. Someone enters the digital scan into the computer program.
   _____

2. The computer program identifies distinctive fingerprint patterns.
   _____

3. The computer program compares the fingerprint patterns against the database.
   _____

4. The computer program identifies matches with fingerprints in the data system.
   _____

5. Detectives use the fingerprint information to identify suspects.
   _____

6. Detectives can use the fingerprint analysis as evidence.
   _____

Exercise D

There is a specific process that investigators must follow when investigating a crime scene. They need to make sure the scene is safe to enter and then keep others away while they talk to the people involved to find out what happened. They then find and collect evidence.

The following paragraph describes the process of investigating a crime scene. It is out of order. First, order the sentences a–h from 1 (first) to 8 (last). Write the number of the order on the line. Then, write a sequencing word on each numbered blank.

| finally | then | once | then |
| next step | the first | to begin | |

_____ a) The $_1$_____ is to interview the victims. Victims can provide a lot of important information such as where the burglars gained access and where missing items were located.

_____ b) When the police get a call informing them of a burglary they must follow a set of established guidelines.

_____ c) Once the police have this information, they target their search to find the right evidence. They search for fibres, fingerprints, hair, and footprints. They start where the burglar entered because that is where the most evidence is. Police $_2$_____ follow the path that the thief likely took based on the items that are missing.

_____ d) $_3$_____, when the police are confident that all possible evidence has been collected, they leave the crime scene.

_____ e) $_4$_____ the evidence has been found, it is carefully stored in clean, sterile envelopes. All evidence is carefully recorded and each stage of the investigation is photographed.

_____ f) $_5$_____thing that they do when they arrive on the scene is to search every room to make sure that the burglar is not there still.

_____ g) $_6$_____ they secure the crime scene. They do this by moving the victims from the scene to a different area and making sure no one enters the premises. They mark the crime scene with yellow tape to block anyone from entering and possibly contaminating the evidence.

_____ h) $_7$_____, police approach a crime scene with caution

Exercise E

Write process paragraphs for 1) securing your home and 2) how the fingerprint database system works. Use the information in Exercises B and C. Add a topic sentence and sequencing words/phrases to make the process clear.

Exercise F

Read the following conversation between a police officer and a shopper. Using the information from the conversation, write a paragraph about how to spot counterfeit items.

Shopper: I got scammed when I bought a designer bag in an online auction. It looked real in the pictures and the seller said it was authentic, but when I got it, I found out it was a fake. Can you give me some suggestions on how I can make sure that the designer handbag I am purchasing is authentic?

Officer: The first thing you should do is go to the designer's website and study pictures of their bags. Look at the designs. Many designers have certain things that they always do. For example, Coach purses always have pairs of CCs stamped in the design—a C never appears on its own.

Shopper: The picture on the auction website looked just like the one on the designer's website.

Officer: That can be a problem if the scammers use a stock photo. You need to see a real picture—actually I wouldn't advise you to buy online. You need to check the materials. Designer bags are always made with expensive materials. The colour of the leather should be consistent. Smell it. You should be able to smell the leather.

Shopper: So if the material appears thin or cheap or smells like plastic, then the purse is not authentic?

Officer: Yeah, that's right. The craftsmanship on high-end purses is superb. Check the stitching for loose threads or sloppy stitching. Check for evidence of glue. Cheap knock-offs often glue the seams together before they sew them. Manufacturers of authentic purses never use glue. You should always check the purse's hardware too. The zippers, buckles, clasps, pulls, and buttons on real designer purses are always very sturdy.

Shopper: The zipper on the bag I bought broke within a week. My big bargain wasn't a bargain at all.

Officer: Another thing to check is the purse's lining. Fakes usually don't use high quality lining that suits the bag. Check the description of the designer's website—they usually describe the pattern of the lining.

Shopper: The style of the bag I purchased is supposed to have brown lining with the designers initials printed all over it. I wish I had done my homework first.

Officer: The purse's logo and label are another way to tell if it is real or fake. In knock-offs, there are often mistakes in the symbol. The scammers try to make it look the same, but in knock-offs there are small differences.

Shopper: I read that you should also check to make sure that the bag's identification number is on a strip of material inside a pocket or main compartment of the bag. The manufacturer sews the brand name into the purse. The purse I bought had a cardboard label hanging off the strap. I know that authentic purses never have cheap labels like that. Is there anything else I should know about?

Officer: Check the packaging. Most designer purses come with dust bags. Confirm that the dust bag and the packaging are the same as what the brand normally provides.

Shopper: Thanks for all the great tips. I guess the most obvious one is location of course. Even I know never to buy a high-end purse from a street vendor.

✓ Process Paragraph Checklist

Content

☐ Does my topic sentence indicate the process that will be explained?

☐ Have I defined and explained unfamiliar terms?

☐ Have I included all the necessary steps in the process?

☐ Have I warned the reader of any difficulties?

☐ Does my concluding sentence draw the reader's attention to the topic sentence again?

Organization

☐ Is the information in the paragraph organized in chronological order?

Meaning

☐ Have I used appropriate transitions?

☐ Have I used precise words to communicate my meaning?

Mechanics

☐ Have I checked my paragraph for mistakes in grammar, spelling, and punctuation?

Academic Word List

analysis	index	previously
approximately	investigation	remove
evidence	occurred	
image	period	

Word Meaning

Exercise A

For each of the following sentences, choose the correct meaning of the underlined word.

1. The blood splatter <u>analysis</u> showed that the victim had been stabbed from behind. The lab technicians studied the shape and size of the spatters.
   a) detailed examination
   b) photographs
   c) description

2. The police determined that the crime occurred at <u>approximately</u> 10 o'clock. The crime may have occurred shortly before or after the estimated time.
   a) exactly
   b) around
   c) precisely

3. Police gathered insect eggs and a few maggots from the body. Based on this <u>evidence</u>, they estimate that the victim was killed about 12 hours ago.
   a) confession by a person
   b) something taken by the criminal
   c) facts that makes you believe something is true

4. A sketch artist drew an <u>image</u> of the suspect based on the eyewitnesses' descriptions. It was really lifelike.
   a) photograph
   b) picture
   c) statue

5. That special computer program has an <u>index</u> of everyone who has been arrested. The police search it to match descriptions of suspects to descriptions of known criminals.
   a) computer code
   b) picture
   c) detailed list

6. The <u>investigation</u> will continue until the crime is solved.
   a) fingerprints and blood evidence
   b) examination of facts
   c) conclusions based on facts

7. The robbery <u>occurred</u> sometime last night.
   a) took place
   b) finished
   c) stole

8. There was a <u>period</u> from January to March when the police thought John was the thief.
   a) a few days
   b) historical time
   c) particular length of time

9. This was not his first arrest. He was <u>previously</u> arrested for break and enter and armed robbery.
   a) after this time
   b) before this time
   c) soon

10. If you <u>remove</u> the beard from the man's face, the sketch looks just like Peter. Peter doesn't have a beard.
    a) colour
    b) add
    c) take away

Pronunciation
Exercise B
Listen to your teacher or an audio dictionary to hear the pronunciation of each word in the list. Repeat each word aloud. Mark the syllables and major word stress.

1. analysis (n)   a / **nál** / y / sis
2. approximately (adv)   _____
3. estimate (v)   _____
4. image (n)   _____
5. index (n)   _____
6. investigation (n)   _____
7. occurred (v)   _____
8. period (n)   _____
9. previously (adv)   _____
10. remove (v)   _____

Word Forms
Exercise C
Fill in the blank with the word form indicated in parentheses. Select only word forms that have the same meaning as in Exercise A.

1. analysis (n): _____ (v)
   _____ (adj)

2. approximately (adv): _____ (adj)
   _____ (n)

3. estimate (v): _____ (n)
   _____ (adj)
   _____ (n)

4. image (n): _____ (n)
   _____ (v)
   _____ (adj)

5. index (n): _____ (v)

6. investigation (n): _____ (v)
   _____ (adj)

7. occur (v): _____ (n)

8. period (n): _____ (adv)

   _____ (adj)

9. previously (adv): _____ (adj)

10. remove (v): _____ (n)

    _____ (adj)

Exercise D

In a dictionary, find one example sentence for each word in Exercise A and copy it into your notebook. Write a second sentence of your own. Then, work with a partner to revise and edit your sentences.

Vocabulary in Context

Exercise E

Read the following paragraph and complete each blank with one of the words from the list. Use each word only once.

analysis	index	previously
approximately	investigation	removed
evidence	occurred	
image	period	

The first theft of the famous painting *The Scream* by Edvard Munch ₁_____ in 1994 during the Winter Olympics in Lillehammer, Norway. *The Scream* is the ₂_____ of a bald person standing on a bridge holding his hands to his face while he screams. Two thieves broke in through a window and ₃_____ the painting. They left behind some important ₄_____—a note that said, "Thank you for the poor security." ₅_____ three months later, the Norwegian government was approached by a group offering to return the painting for $1 million. The government didn't pay. Instead, they participated in an ₆_____ with the British police for a ₇_____ of seven months. After a careful ₈_____ of all the evidence, they were able to locate the painting and bring it back to the museum.

In 2004, the same painting that had been stolen 10 years ₉_____ was stolen again. The robbers carried guns. They also took another Munch painting. It took two years for the Norwegian police to find the painting. The methods the police used to find the paintings have not been revealed. Perhaps they were able to find some DNA evidence at the scene and run it through CODIS (Combined DNA ₁₀_____ System). Or, perhaps they just got lucky. This probably won't be the last time that thieves attempt to steal this famous painting.

Unit 7
Doing the Right Thing

Vocabulary

Exercise A
Fill in the blanks with words from the list below.

accountable	corruption	illegally
behaviour	fair	unethical
cheating	guilty	
consequences	harm	

Police arrested a local government employee yesterday on charges of 1 _____. Samuel Madison has worked in the city's home-building department for the last fifteen years. Madison has been accused of various 2 _____ business practices including, bribery, forgery, and fraud. He may have acted 3 _____ by accepting money for years from builders in exchange for approving home-building permits. The city has strict rules for building houses. Some of the building designs that he approved did not follow local building rules. This has had serious 4 _____. Some homeowners have had to pay a lot of money to replace roofs, rebuild walls, and fix other construction problems. In one situation, a man died when his house collapsed as a result of a mistake in architectural design. Madison had approved the design without checking that the architect had followed the proper building rules. Madison is also accused of signing the names of other government officials on important documents without their knowledge. The head of the government department where Madison works has called

Madison's 5 _____ immoral. "This man has been 6 _____ taxpayers out of a lot of money for years," the leader said. "He has caused a lot of 7 _____ and he must be held 8 _____ for his actions." If Madison is found 9 _____, he will spend several years in jail. According to several of his victims, that would be 10 _____ considering his unacceptable behaviour.

Exercise B
Use the hints at the end of the lines to write one word that fits both blanks. Use each word only once.

accountable	ethical	legal
behaviour	fair	lie
cheat	guilty	steal
consequences	harmful	
corruption	honest	

EXAMPLE: <u>stolen</u> property, <u>stolen</u> jewellery
        adjective   adjective

1. rewarded for good _____; punished
                          noun
for bad _____ (hint: actions)
         noun

2. police _____; government
          noun
_____
noun
(hint: dishonest actions by people in power)

3. serious _____; negative
       plural noun
_____ (hint: outcomes)
plural noun

4. _____ document;
    adjective
_____ advice
   adjective
(hint: according to the law)

5. an _____ mistake; an
       adjective
   _____ living
       adjective
   (hint: without the intention of doing something wrong)

6. _____ problem;
       adjective
   _____ dilemma
       adjective
   (hint: concerning right and wrong actions)

7. feel _____; look
        adverb
   _____
       adverb
   (hint: knowing you have done something wrong)

8. _____ trial; _____
       adjective   adjective
   treatment (hint: objective and equitable)

9. _____ effects;
       adjective
   _____ consequences (hint: hurtful)
       adjective

10. _____ money;
        verb
    _____ an idea
        verb
    (hint: take something that is not yours)

11. _____ for your decisions;
        adjective
    _____ for your actions
        adjective
    (hint: responsible)

12. detect a _____; tell a
                 noun
    _____ (hint: untruth)
        noun

13. _____ on a test;
        verb
    _____ on your boyfriend or
        verb
    girlfriend (hint: be dishonest to get what you want)

Vocabulary Expansion

Prefixes that mean "not" or "the opposite of"
un-, **dis-**, **il-** (also **in-**, **ir-**, **im-**)

Exercise C

In each sentence the italicized word has the wrong prefix. Write the correct prefix. Look up the underlined root word in a dictionary to help you.

1. Christine is very *ilorganized*, so she gets confused easily. _____

2. I read about the corrupt police officer with *unbelief*. _____

3. If a student feels she has been treated *infairly*, she has a right to make a formal complaint. _____

4. If government leaders are *iraccountable* to the public, it is easier for them to use their power for personal benefit instead of for the public good. _____

5. In Canada, it is *unlegal* to not report all your income to the government. _____

6. It is *unpossible* to build a strong economy when businesses and the government are corrupt. _____

7. Milan is a very *disresponsible* man. He is constantly making bad choices. _____

8. Most people believe that killing another person is *unmoral*. _____

9. She divorced her husband because of his *unhonesty*. _____

10. The CFO (chief financial officer) was fired because of his *illoyalty* to the company. _____

11. Too much guilt can be psychologically and physically *imhealthy*. _____

12. We have laws to protect people from *inethical* practices. _____

13. Your actions are not *disconsequential* because they affect what happens in the future. _____

14. Your reason for making this harmful decision is *dislogical*. It doesn't make sense. _____

Exercise D

The prefixes **dis-**, **un-**, **il-**, **in-**, **im-**, or **ir-** give the meaning "not" to the main word; however, not all words that begin with these letters use them as a prefix. For example, the word **in**dustry begins with the letters **in-**, but these letters are not a prefix to a main word.

In each list of words on the next page, four words use **dis-**, **un-**, **il-**, **in-**, **im-**, or **ir-** as a prefix that means "not," and three words do not. Underline the words with the prefix "not."

1. image   immigrate   impatient   imperfect
   impersonal   imply   impossible

2. disagree   disapprove   discuss   disease
   dissatisfaction distinct   distrust

3. unafraid   unbelievable   uncertain   uncle
   united   unique   unusual

4. income   independent   indicate   insecure
   individual   inessential   informal

5. illegal   illiterate   illness   illogical
   illegitimate illusion   illustration

6. iron   irrational   irregular   irrelevant
   irreplaceable irritate   irate

Grammar Focus

Unreal and Real Conditionals

Exercise A

Match the conditions to the results.

Condition	Result
a) If you lied to me,	1. she'd be stealing.
b) If I lied on my job application,	2. I wouldn't have to ask for your advice.
c) If elected government officials didn't treat people fairly,	3. I wouldn't lie to protect him.
d) If the student were caught cheating on a test,	4. I'd be upset with you.
e) If I knew he had committed a crime and the police asked me about it,	5. she would get a grade of zero.
f) If I already knew what to do,	6. it wouldn't be fair to other applicants.
g) If society didn't have laws to punish us when we behave badly,	7. people wouldn't vote for them.
h) If she had to choose between right and wrong,	8. she'd choose to do the right thing.
i) If he broke the law,	9. we wouldn't act ethically.
j) If she took the money from his wallet without asking,	10. he would get arrested.

Exercise B

Fill in the blanks with the correct tense to signal whether you think the conditional sentence is real (possible) or unreal (impossible or unlikely).

1. Generally, people _____ (treat) you with respect, if you _____ (be) respectful of them.

2. If a teacher _____ (catch) a student cheating, she _____ (take) his paper and _____ (give) him a failing grade.

3. If a doctor _____ (publish) a patient's medical information on the Internet, the patient _____ (can sue) the doctor.

4. If your teacher _____ (ask) you for a bribe to pass the course, the school _____ (fire) him.

5. If a landlord _____ (not rent) you an apartment because of your skin colour, the landlord _____ (break) the law.

6. An employer _____ (have) the right to fire a worker, if the worker _____ (steal) from the company.

7. If your father _____ (hit) a pedestrian with his car and _____ (leave) the scene of the accident, the police _____ (look) for him and _____ (arrest) him.

8. If your neighbour _____ (set) fire to your house, he _____ (go) to jail.

9. In Canada, if a husband _____ (beat) his wife, he _____ (break) the law.

10. If a scam artist _____ (cheat) me out of $1000, I _____ (feel) very angry.

Exercise C

What would be the consequences of the following actions?

1. If she cheated on her exam, _____

2. If she didn't cheat on the exam, _____

3. If everyone downloaded music without paying for it, _____

4. If students never download music without paying for it, _____
5. If people never lied to others, _____
6. If people always lied to others, _____
7. If no businesses were corrupt, _____
8. If all businesses were corrupt, _____
9. If people were free to do anything they wanted, _____
10. If people had no freedom to do what they wanted, _____

Exercise D

Use your imagination. Write four "if" sentences for each situation.

1. Imagine a world without the Internet.
   a) _____
   b) _____
   c) _____
   d) _____

2. Imagine a world without birds.
   a) _____
   b) _____
   c) _____
   d) _____

3. Imagine a world without schools.
   a) _____
   b) _____
   c) _____
   d) _____

4. Imagine a world in which everyone looked the same.
   a) _____
   b) _____
   c) _____
   d) _____

Grammar Edit

In each opinion below there is an error in (a) punctuation, (b) verb form, or (c) clause pattern. Find the one mistake in each sentence and fix it.

1. Crime will go down if Canada had the death penalty.
2. Fewer students would finish high school, if a high school education wasn't free.
3. If actions did have not consequences, ethics wouldn't matter.
4. If businesses run health care instead of the government, Canada would have better health care.
5. Workers didn't be motivated to work well if companies didn't reward them with good pay.
6. If gay marriages weren't legal in Canada people would be less tolerant of a gay lifestyle.
7. If religion didn't exist, people still behave ethically.
8. If someone in my family would stole a car, I would lie to the police to protect them.
9. If the government ban smoking altogether, the cost of health care would go down.
10. If didn't treat laws people fairly, people would demonstrate.
11. It wouldn't be fair, if some students were punished for plagiarizing while others were not.
12. It wouldn't be fair if had to retire women earlier than men.

Reading

Guided Summary

A summary is a short, concise piece of writing that requires you to put the main points of the reading in your own words. It is always shorter than the original reading.

Write a summary of the two different opinions in the reading about music piracy on pages 85–86 in the Student Book. Use the questions on the next page as a guide.

Music Piracy: Is Downloading Music Ethical?
Joost Steffensen

In order to persuade his readers to support his opinion about the ethics of downloading music, he tries to disprove some common arguments against illegal downloading.

Paragraph B:	1. What is the writer's main idea?
	2. What is his reasoning?
Paragraphs C and E:	3. What is one common argument against free music downloading?
	4. How can artists make money even when their music is downloaded for free?
Paragraph G:	5. What is one problem with the movie and music industries?
Paragraphs H and I:	6. What is another problem with companies in the music industry?
	7. Give one example of the problem.
Paragraph K:	8. What should the music industry do?
Paragraph L:	9. What should users do in the meantime?

Leigh Goessl

The writer argues that the facts that people who support illegal music downloading give to justify their actions are not the important ethical considerations. She states what the important ethical problems really are.

Paragraphs A and B:	1. What is the writer's main idea?
	2. What is her reasoning?
Paragraph D:	3. The problem isn't that people don't know downloading music for free is wrong. What don't people understand according to the writer?
Paragraph E:	4. What is one common comparison that supporters of illegal music downloading make?
	5. Give one reason this is not a good comparison.
Paragraph F:	6. What does the writer think about the attractiveness of illegal music downloading?
Paragraphs F to H:	7. What is another common argument people make in favour of downloading music without paying for it?
	8. Who has the right to decide whether people should be able to download and why?
Paragraph J:	9. Why do people not think about the consequences of their illegal downloading activities?
Paragraph K:	10. What must people realize?

Writing

Model Paragraph

College students know that cheating is unethical. So, why do students still cheat? Cheating is not simply a matter of personal choice. Excessive pressure to succeed, peer acceptance of cheating, and poor
5 teaching all cause students to cheat. One reason students cheat is that there are many unrealistically high expectations for them to succeed. In the workplace, success is rewarded and measured in dollars. In education, success is rewarded and
10 measured in grades. When students' grades are low, however, parents get angry, teachers are disappointed, and peers often look down on them. In order to avoid embarrassment and failure, students go to great lengths to get high marks, and that often includes
15 cheating. Another cause of cheating is peer acceptance of cheating. Everybody knows someone who has cheated. Even in the workplace, in politics, and in government, some people cheat to get ahead. When

"everybody does it," cheating becomes acceptable.
25 Once you believe that everybody cheats, you feel that you have to cheat too just to keep up. More importantly, once you believe everyone cheats, you don't feel guilty about cheating. A final cause of cheating is poor teaching. Of course, teachers
30 shouldn't make the class work or tests too easy, but sometimes class work or tests are unfair. The test questions might be worded to deliberately trick the students. Students will think this is unfair. When a teacher is unfair or too harsh, it results in cheating. If you think that students cheat mainly because they're too lazy to study, think again. Pressure to be successful, acceptance of cheating by others, and poor teaching all result in student cheating.

1. What is the writer's aim in this paragraph?
2. What is the topic of this paragraph? Underline the sentence that tells what this paragraph is about.
3. How many different points does the writer make in exploring the topic?
4. How are the points ordered? In order of familiarity? In order of importance? In order of time?
5. What kind of information does the writer use to support each of the points? Examples, explanations, definitions, statistics?

> **Cause-and-Effect Paragraphs**
> In cause-and-effect paragraphs writers analyze the causes or effects of a thing in order to understand it. Causes explain why something happens. Effects explain the results of something happening. In shorter paragraphs, writers explore only causes or only effects, not both. The causes or effects in the paragraph are usually ordered from most important, interesting, or familiar to least important, interesting, or familiar. Sometimes cause / effect paragraphs show the writer's opinions. In such cases, the writer is trying to persuade the reader to agree with the causes or effects. Other times they only give information and the writer stays neutral.

Exercise A

In each sentence, circle the word or phrase that connects a cause-and-effect relationship. Then, identify if what follows is a cause (C) or an effect (E).

___1. Businesses lose about $600 billion every year as a result of employee theft and fraud in the workplace.

___2. Because of the high accident rate of young male drivers, car insurance for this group is more expensive than for older drivers or female drivers.

___3. His parents raised him to be honest and respectful. Consequently, he acted with honour and integrity in all his business deals.

___4. Having clear rules and consequences for good and bad behaviour leads to ethical behaviour.

___5. Some customers buy clothes from a clothing store, wear them for a short time with the tags tucked in, and then return them for a full refund; this kind of consumer fraud results in losses of about $16 billion a year for the retail industry.

___6. Corruption in business and government results from greed and the desire for power.

___7. Bribery is illegal. Therefore, bribery must be punished.

___8. The workers became angry and resentful since the boss hired his son and nephew for the two new positions in the department.

___9. The school's reputation for closing an eye to student cheating caused many businesses to stop hiring its graduates.

___10. Parents get angry when children come home with bad grades, so children will cheat to get higher grades.

Words and Phrases That Connect Causes and Effects

Cause X	Effect Y
as a result of + ... *noun or gerund (phrase)*	consequently
because of + ... *noun or gerund (phrase)*	as a result
	therefore
because + s + v ...	lead to (v) + ... *noun or gerund (phrase)*
result from (v) + ... *noun or gerund (phrase)*	result in (v) + ... *noun or gerund (phrase)*
since	cause (v)
	so

Y (is true / happens) as a result of X
Y results from X
Y (is true / happens) because / because of X
Y (is true / happens) since X
X causes Y
X leads to Y
X (is true). Therefore, Y
X (is true / happens). Consequently, Y
X results in Y
X (is true / happens), so Y (is true / happens)
X happens. As a result, Y happens.

Exercise B

Fill in the blank with an appropriate *cause* or *effect* word(s) from the list above. Use each word only once. More than one answer may be possible.

1. A high neighbourhood crime rate will _____ businesses leaving the area.
2. Treating employees unfairly _____ workers to resent company managers.
3. Amnesty International criticized the country _____ its humanrights abuses.
4. As northern countries get warmer, insects that carry diseases will move north. _____ diseases will spread to these areas.
5. Poverty _____ poorer health.
6. Children copy the behaviour of people they love and admire, _____ it's important for parents to behave ethically.
7. Good psychological health in children _____ a loving and caring family life.
8. _____ family life has a strong influence on physical and emotional health, it is important for parents to provide a loving and caring environment in the home.

Exercise C

List three causes to answer each question.

EXAMPLE: What causes students to cheat on exams?
- pressure to succeed
- peer acceptance of cheating
- poor teaching

1. What causes some people to lie on a job application?
   _____
   _____

2. What causes children to lie to their parents?
   _____
   _____

3. What causes some companies to ignore pollution laws?
   _____
   _____

4. What causes some people to shoplift*?
   _____
   _____

*take products from a shop without paying for them

List three effects to answer each question. You may choose to write about negative effects or positive effects.

EXAMPLE: What are the possible effects of working illegally?
- Workers may have to work for very low wages.
- Workers may have to work in unsafe conditions.
- People may think illegal workers will break other laws too.

1. What are the possible effects of ignoring student cheating?
   _____
   _____
   _____

2. What are the possible effects of not punishing bribery?
   _____
   _____
   _____

3. What are the possible effects of lowering entrance standards for colleges and universities?
   _____
   _____
   _____

4. What are the possible effects of legalizing same-sex marriages?
   _____
   _____
   _____

Exercise D

Write sentences to show the cause-and-effect relationships in Exercise C.

Exercise E

Read the outline for each cause-or-effect paragraph.

a) Write C if the paragraph is about causes of the situation or E if it is about effects.

b) Write a topic sentence for each paragraph that includes
   - the topic;
   - a focus on either the causes or effects of the situation; and
   - a brief list of the causes or effects the paragraph explores.

c) Write the paragraph for one of the outlines.

EXAMPLE: Working illegally
   - very low wages
   - work in unsafe conditions
   - illegal workers will break other laws

a) **E:** this paragraph explores the effects of working illegally.

b) **Topic sentence:** Working illegally often results in low wages and unsafe working conditions for workers and may lead others to believe these workers will break other laws too.

c) **Paragraph:** Working illegally often results in low wages and unsafe working conditions for workers and may lead others to believe these workers will break other laws too. The most common result of working illegally is that employers pay illegal workers much less than employees who work for them legally. This makes it hard for illegal workers to make a better life. Another serious effect of working illegally is that workers may have to work in an unsafe workplace. People who work illegally are not protected by the laws that force companies to be safe and illegal workers will not get any insurance money for injuries. Finally, when people work illegally others may not trust them. They may believe that since a worker is agreeing to break the law to work without proper documents, he or she will agree to break the law in other situations too. Some people think that working illegally benefits the worker because working is better than not working, but working illegally has many bad effects.

1. Accepting bribes
   - greed and selfishness; want personal benefits without earning them
   - want power; accepting gift in exchange for a favour shows you have power
   - don't think bribery is wrong; if others offer and take bribes, it becomes normal and acceptable.

2. Government censorship of information on the Internet
   - citizens don't have full information about what is happening; easier to control what people think
   - protects children from accessing pornography
   - controls problem of Internet predators; can reduce crime
   - helps keep social order; shut down information that is harmful or untruthful about government

3. Drinking and driving
   - higher car insurance rates for everyone; unfair
   - lose driver's licence; problem for workers who drive for work
   - more deaths; families of victims devastated

Exercise F

Make an outline with a topic sentence for one of the topics in Exercises C or D. Then write a paragraph from your outline. Use the Cause-and-Effect Paragraph Checklist to edit your work.

✅ Cause-and-Effect Paragraph Checklist

Content

☐ Is it clear that my purpose is **either**
  a) to understand the causes or effects of an event or situation (analysis); **or**
  b) to convince the reader that my particular perspective on the causes or effects is true (opinion)?

☐ Does my topic sentence clearly state a focus on either causes or effects?

☐ Are the causes or effects I have presented based on a logical analysis of the event or situation?

☐ Do all my statements connect to the focus stated in the topic sentence?

☐ Have I ensured that the causes and effects are sufficiently but briefly explained?

☐ Does my concluding sentence draw the reader's attention to the topic sentence again?

Organization

☐ Is the information in the paragraph organized in a logical way: in order of importance or in order of familiarity?

☐ Have I used words or phrases that show how the ideas are ordered: *one* (noun), *a second* (noun), *another* (noun), *the most important* (noun), etc.?

Meaning

☐ Have I used cause-and-effect words or phrases properly to show the cause-and-effect relationships within sentences (*because of*, *results in*, etc.)?

☐ Have I used cause-and-effect words or phrases properly to show the relationship between sentences (*therefore*, *consequently*, etc.)?

☐ Have I used precise words to communicate my meaning?

Mechanics

☐ Have I checked my paragraph for mistakes in grammar, spelling, and punctuation?

Academic Word List

available	consumer	tape
commit	distribute	technique
compute	final	
conclusion	focus	

Word Meaning
Exercise A

Read the examples for the word in bold. Then, choose the meaning for the word.

1. Killers **commit** murder.
   People who are severely depressed may **commit** suicide.
   A married person **commits** adultery when having a love affair outside the marriage.

   commit (v):
   a) to think a bad and unpopular thought
   b) to disagree with the rules of society
   c) to do something wrong or illegal

2. Banks make money **available** to customers.
   Libraries make books **available** to borrowers.
   Concert tickets are **available** to patrons at the box office.

   available (adj):
   a) possible to get and use
   b) possible to sell and buy
   c) possible to cancel

3. Companies design **consumer** products with users in mind.
   You can protect yourself from **consumer** fraud by keeping your financial and personal information private.
   Consumer demand for oil is increasing.

   consumer (adj):
   a) something for or by the people who buy goods and services for their own use
   b) something for or by the people who provide products and services for others
   c) something for or by the people who make advertisements for products and services

4. International companies **distribute** their products to stores throughout the world.
   In public elementary schools, teachers **distribute** books to all their students.
   Publishers **distribute** newspapers to thousands of readers through home delivery.

   distribute (v):
   a) to supply to many people or places
   b) to sell to many people or places
   c) to make for many people or places

5. After studying the evidence at a crime scene carefully, police can draw a **conclusion** about who committed the crime.
   Cancer researchers came to the **conclusion** years ago that smoking causes cancer.
   It can take a long time for a jury to reach a **conclusion** about a person's innocence or guilt.

   conclusion (n):
   a) to make a guess
   b) to make a judgment based on reason
   c) to be uncertain

6. Music used to be available on audio **tape**, but now we have CDs.
   Movies used to be recorded on video **tape**, but now we have DVDs.
   Computer data used to be recorded on **tape**, but this is an old technology.

   tape (n):
   a) a technology where only sound and film could be stored on plastic, but not other information
   b) a technology that had only mechanical parts which did not allow films to be recorded
   c) a technology where information was stored on a thin, narrow ribbon with a magnetic cover

7. Photographers **focus** their cameras on what they want to photograph.
   Learners of English need to **focus** on spelling when they write, but not when they speak.
   Writers **focus** on words whereas mathematicians **focus** on numbers.

   focus (v):
   a) to pay special attention to
   b) to use a lot
   c) to have some skill

8. An artist uses a different **technique** to create an oil painting than to create a pencil drawing.
   Manufacturing **techniques** used to be based on mechanical technology, but today they are based on computer technology.
   Using a wok is a popular Asian cooking **technique** that is not common in Western cooking.

   technique (n):
   a) a special technology
   b) a skillful way to do something
   c) a strong desire

9. Students often use calculators to **compute** answers to math questions.
   Physicists **compute** distances in space.
   Accountants **compute** how much tax companies must pay to the government.

   compute (v):
   a) to calculate
   b) to answer
   c) to study

10. Researchers make a **final** conclusion only after much careful study.
    In court, a judge's decision is **final**.
    Some people think that the **final** choice about whom to marry should be the individual's while others believe it should be the family's.

    final (adj):
    a) shows that something is ethical and cannot be different
    b) shows that something is good and cannot be decided by someone else
    c) shows that something is decided and cannot be argued against

Pronunciation
Exercise B

Listen to your teacher or an audio dictionary to hear the pronunciation for each word in the list. Repeat each word aloud. Mark the syllables and major word stress.

1. available (adj)   a / **vail** / a / ble
2. commit (v)   _____
3. computer (v)   _____
4. conclusion (v)   _____
5. consumer (v)   _____

6. distribute (v) _____
7. final (adj) _____
8. focus (v) _____
9. tape (n) _____
10. technique (n) _____

Word Forms

Exercise C

Fill in the blank with the word form shown in parentheses. More than one word may be possible for each word form. Select only word forms that have the same meaning as in Exercise A.

1. available (adj): _____ (n)
2. commit (v):
3. compute (v): _____ (n)
4. conclusion (n): _____ (v)
   _____ (adj)
5. consumer (adj): _____ (n)
   _____ (n)
   _____ (v)
6. distribute (v): _____ (n)
   _____ (n)
7. final (adj): _____ (adv)
8. focus (v): _____ (n)
   _____ (adj)
9. tape (n): _____ (v)
10. technique (n)

Exercise D

In a dictionary, find one example sentence for each word in Exercise A and copy it into your notebook. Write a second sentence of your own. Then, work with a partner to revise and edit your sentences.

Exercise E

Read the story and complete each blank with a word from the list. Use each word only once.

| available | distributed | techniques |
| computer | taping | |

Last year, a friend of mine was the victim of extreme bullying by an ex-boyfriend. Bullying occurs when a person with greater power in a relationship repeatedly harasses a person with lesser power. Jane's ex-boyfriend, John, used to work for the same company as she did. They dated for about three months. John was becoming more and more controlling, so Jane decided to end the relationship. That's when the real trouble started. John used several different ₁_____ to harass Jane. He installed a virus onto Jane's ₂_____ at home. It crashed and she lost all her information. He also stole photos of Jane and ₃_____ them to their co-workers anonymously. The photos weren't very nice. They showed Jane drinking (a lot) at parties and dancing wildly. They weren't terrible photos, but they certainly weren't photos she wanted her colleagues and boss to see. Even her parents and clients saw the photos after John posted them online, which made them ₄_____ for everyone to see. Another way he harassed her was by phoning her and ₅_____ the conversation—not on cassette of course, but with a digital recorder. He said mean things. She got upset and said mean things back. Then he threatened to make her comments public. That's when she called the police.

| committing | focuses | final |
| conclusion | consumers | |

The police explained that John was actually ₆_____ a crime by harassing her. The police could charge him and take him to court. If the court came to the ₇_____ that

John was guilty, he would be punished. Jane didn't want to punish John. She just wanted the bullying to stop. I disagreed with her and advised her to lay charges. I work for the Office of Consumer Affairs, a government agency that $_8$ _____ on protecting $_9$ _____ from unethical business practices. My specialty is computer privacy. I know that if you ignore criminal behaviour, you encourage it. Society can have all kinds of laws to protect people and agencies to enforce the laws, but the $_{10}$ _____ responsibility for holding business, government, and private citizens accountable for their behaviour lies with individuals. So, John was charged with harassment, he was fired from his job, and he is, by law, not allowed to contact Jane anymore.

Unit 8
Love Is in the Air

Vocabulary

Exercise A
Complete the crossword using the words below.

caring	manipulative	respectful
controlling	mature	responsible
honest	obsessive	stubborn
humorous	outgoing	trustworthy
jealous	reliable	

Across

1. Someone who shows kindness and concern for others is …
3. Someone who behaves like an adult is …
6. Someone who shows politeness and honour toward another person is …
7. Someone who tells the truth is …
8. Someone who thinks about one thing or one person all the time is …
10. Someone who won't change their opinions about the way they do things is …
11. Someone who makes good judgements and is trustworthy is…
12. Someone who is funny is …
13. Someone who tries to influence other people to do things that benefit himself is …

Down

1. Someone who tells you what to do all the time is …
2. Someone who is unhappy about something you have and they want is …
4. Someone who behaves as you expect them to is …
5. Someone who is energetic and friendly toward others is …
9. Someone whom you can believe will be good and won't let you down is …

Exercise B
Circle the word in each set that has a similar meaning to the word in bold.

1. **caring**   a) considerate   b) honest
2. **controlling**   a) bossy   b) irresponsible
3. **honest**   a) truthful   b) mature
4. **jealous**   a) obsessive   b) envious
5. **mature**   a) responsible   b) spontaneous
6. **manipulative** a) unfair   b) cunning
7. **obsessive**   a) fanatical   b) irresponsible
8. **outgoing**   a) sociable   b) trustworthy
9. **reliable**   a) concerned   b) dependable
10. **respectful**   a) concerned   b) polite
11. **responsible** a) concerned   b) conscientious
12. **stubborn**   a) inflexible   b) critical
13. **trustworthy** a) reliable   b) kind
14. **humorous**   a) concerned   b) funny

73

Vocabulary Expansion

Exercise C

The prefixes **dis-**, **im-**, **ir-**, and **un-** can be placed before adjectives to mean "not" or "the opposite of." The following personality traits are positive. Write the correct prefix to make the meaning negative.

1. ____ agreeable
2. ____ caring
3. ____ controllable
4. ____ ethical
5. ____ honest
6. ____ mature
7. ____ moral
8. ____ pleasant
9. ____ polite
10. ____ predictable
11. ____ rational
12. ____ respectful
13. ____ responsible
14. ____ trustful
15. ____ trustworthy

Exercise D

Complete the blanks to make a word from Exercise C.

1. He does not honour his elders. He is dis _____ of older people.
2. He always argues with other people. He's quite dis _____.
3. He doesn't make good decisions. He's ir _____.
4. He is not concerned with other people. He is un _____.
5. He is not nice to people. He is un _____.
6. He acts like a child. He is im _____.
7. You never know what he's going to do or say. He's un _____.
8. She is not a logical thinker. She's ir _____.
9. You can't trust her. She is un _____.
10. She doesn't trust others. She is dis _____.
11. She knows the difference between right and wrong, but she does what is wrong anyway. She is im _____.
12. She can't stop feeling angry. Her anger is un _____.
13. She lies and cheats all the time. She is dis _____.
14. She's not just im _____ She's rude.
15. She does not behave in a moral way. She is un _____.

Grammar Focus

Adjective Clauses
Exercise A

Complete the sentence with an appropriate pronoun and the correct form of the verb in parentheses.

EXAMPLE: A marriage _____ (pronoun) _____ (be) based in friendship will last.

A marriage that is based in friendship will last.

1. A marriage _____ (pronoun) _____ (has) a lot of financial stress often ends in divorce.
2. A marriage _____ (pronoun) _____ (not allow) both partners to grow as a couple and as independent people will be unhappy.
3. A woman _____ (pronoun) _____ (think) that she can change the man she marries will be in for a surprise. She can't.
4. Canada has a law _____ (pronoun) _____ (give) homosexual couples the right to marry, so that lesbians and gay men are treated fairly in society.
5. Couples _____ (pronoun) _____ (live) together for a few years, but who are not legally married are protected under the law in Canada. These common-law couples have the same rights and responsibilities as legally married couples.

6. Couples _____ (pronoun) _____ (marry) for love are usually happier than couples in a marriage without love.

7. Group dating may be a good choice for people _____ (pronoun) _____ (be) uncomfortable dating one-to-one.

8. In today's society, men and women _____ (pronoun) _____ (move) to a new town often find it difficult to meet dating partners.

9. Some people believe that couples _____ (pronoun) _____ (have) different cultural backgrounds should not marry.

10. Romantic relationships _____ (pronoun) _____ (begin) online are becoming more and more common.

Exercise B
Rearrange the words below to complete the sentences.

1. humour likes sense people He have
   _____ _____ who _____ a _____ of _____.

2. educated find Her her is parents partner
   _____ _____ want to _____ a _____ who _____.

3. have healthy important is It relationship
   _____ is _____ to _____ a _____ that _____.

4. family have nice peaceful that
   It is _____ to _____ a _____ life _____ is _____.

5. are Jennifer likes romantic
   _____ _____ dates that _____ _____.

6. controlling people want who
   Most _____ don't _____ a partner _____ is _____.

7. has who is wife
   Tim _____ a _____ _____ _____ outgoing.

8. generous is man She
   _____ married a _____ who _____.

9. marriages that have
   Some couples _____ _____ _____ were arranged.

10. are exciting movies prefer They
    _____ _____ _____ that _____ _____.

Exercise C
Combine the following sentences using adjective clauses.

1. Nick has a girlfriend. She is smart.
   _____

2. They went on a date. The date was boring.
   _____

3. He bought her a ring. The ring was very expensive.
   _____

4. They went to a wedding. The wedding was fun.
   _____

5. Tina has a husband. Her husband is easygoing.
   _____

6. They celebrated their wedding in a restaurant. The restaurant was beautifully decorated.
   _____

7. Do you think it's OK for a man to marry a woman? The woman is twenty years younger than him.
_____
_____

8. He was married to a woman. She was manipulative.
_____
_____

Exercise D

Read the sentences. Think about the meaning of the situation. Then, write a sentence with an adjective clause. More than one answer may be possible.

EXAMPLE: *Some engagement rings are too expensive. I don't want that kind of engagement ring.*

I don't want an engagement ring that is too expensive.

1. Mary went on a blind date. It was organized by one of her friends. _____
_____

2. She is writing an online dating profile. Hopefully it will attract suitable partners. _____
_____

3. A guy responded to your online dating profile. Are you going to call him? _____
_____

4. She was dating a young man. He moved here six months ago. Is she still dating him? _____
_____

5. The computer game just came on the market last week. Ben's girlfriend bought him the game. _____
_____

6. When Hatem was a young man, he had to follow old-fashioned dating rules. He thinks it is silly to make his children follow these same rules. _____
_____

7. Do you think it's OK for young people to date? Is it OK if they're still in high school? _____
_____

8. One couple had three children. They were married for 25 years. Another couple had no children. They were married for 10 years. (Which couple was married longer?) _____
_____

Exercise E

Complete the sentences with an adjective clause.

1. I don't like dates … _____
_____

2. Most couples want a wedding …_____
_____

3. Most men don't want a woman … _____
_____

4. Most women don't want a man … _____
_____

5. If you want to have a marriage … _____
_____

6. A marriage has a better chance of succeeding if you have in-laws … _____

7. Couples … _____
are more likely to stay together.

8. People … _____
make good marriage partners.

9. People … _____
can still live happy and productive lives.

10. Marriages … _____
are likely to end in divorce.

Grammar Edit

Read the story and underline the eight adjective clauses. Each adjective clause has a grammar mistake with the structure of the adjective clause. Rewrite the sentence to fix the mistake.

1 Peter and his girlfriend Maya had a terrible date.
2 Peter had planned the date for weeks, but everything
3 went wrong. It wasn't an evening that it was
4 fun or romantic. First of all, Peter had brought
5 Maya a bouquet of mixed flowers. She liked the
6 chrysanthemums, but she was allergic to the roses
7 that in the bouquet were. They made her sneeze all
8 night. Then, they went to a movie theatre. They saw
9 a film about a woman who she fell in love with her

10 neighbour. That part wasn't so bad, but the neighbour
11 was an alcoholic womanizer. Peter thought the movie
12 was terrible. He said the woman was stupid to fall
13 in love with a man who he was a loser. After the
14 movie, they went to a restaurant. The food wasn't
15 very good. Neither Peter nor Maya likes meat who
16 is undercooked. The meat was almost raw, so they
17 sent it back to the kitchen. Vegetables that they are
18 overcooked have no taste. These vegetables were like
19 mush. Maya only picked at them with her fork. It was
20 expensive too. A restaurant that a lot of money charges
21 should have much better food. It was late when they
22 left the restaurant. The subway that it they took broke
23 down. They had to get off the train and take the bus.
24 They both agreed it was a disappointing date.

Reading

Guided Summary

A summary is a short, concise piece of writing that requires you to put the main points of the reading in your own words. It is always shorter than the original reading.

Use the responses to these questions to write a summary paragraph of "On Love and Marriage: The East and West in All of Us" on pages 103–105 in the Student Book.

Background and context:

1. Who is the writer and what is his personal situation?
2. What confused the writer as he was growing up? What is the dilemma?

Details (identifying the main arguments):

3. Who or what influenced the writer's attitude about love? What did he learn about love?
4. Who or what influenced the writer's attitude about marriage? What did he learn about marriage? What arguments explain this point of view about marriage?

Resolution

5. How did the writer's understanding of the dilemma change from childhood into adulthood?
6. How does the writer solve the dilemma for himself? What specifically does he want to do?

If you wish, begin your paragraph this way: "Anand Ram is a young man who grew up in the West, but whose parents and family are from India."

Writing

Model Paragraph

I'm a 28-year-old woman who recently married. At my wedding, my 90-year-old great-grandmother shared with me her own stories about life as a married woman. Traditional marriages like my great-
5 grandmother's differ from modern marriages like my own in very important ways. Firstly, in traditional marriages, women and men had different roles. The man went to work and was responsible for the financial success of the family. The woman, in
10 contrast, stayed home to manage the household and care for the children. All important decisions about money and disciplining children were made by the husband. Secondly, the extended family was very involved in the married life of the couple. Parents
15 decided when and who their children married, especially their daughters. It was not uncommon for a married couple to live with the parents or grandparents of the wife or husband. Finally, in traditional marriages, life was focused on the marriage.
20 The husband may have belonged to an all-male sports club, but the woman's interests were focused on life in the home. She was not expected to develop interests that were not related to her life as a married woman. In modern marriages, on the other hand, the
25 husband and wife share roles. A modern husband also takes care of the children and cleans the house. He wouldn't dream of making a major decision without his wife's agreement. Also, modern couples are much less dependent on their extended family. Parents and
30 grandparents visit and may even live with the couple later in life, but they generally do not give advice until asked. Finally, in modern marriages both the husband and wife lead a life outside the marriage. It is acceptable for them to have interests and friendships

35 outside the marriage and to spend time developing these separately. Of course, there are similarities between traditional and modern marriages, but the differences are significant.

1. What is the writer's aim in this paragraph?
2. What is the topic of this paragraph? Underline the sentence that tells what this paragraph is about.
3. How does the writer organize the comparison points in relation to the topics being compared? Is it point-by-point or all about one, then all about the other?
4. What word(s) are used to show similarities and differences?
5. What words are used to signal transitions between comparison points?

Paragraphs That Compare and Contrast

Comparison-and-contrast paragraphs show similarities and differences between ideas, people, or things. To compare two things, you show how they are similar. To contrast two things, you show how they are different. The two things being compared or contrasted must belong to the same group. For example, you can compare the similarities and differences between traditional and modern marriages because they are both *types of marriages*.

The purpose of writing a contrast or comparison paragraph is to persuade or inform the reader. For example, in a paragraph comparing traditional and modern marriage you might want to persuade the reader that a modern marriage is better for women than a traditional marriage. Or, you might want to provide information to the reader that simply shows in what ways modern and traditional marriages are different.

Exercise A

When you compare or contrast two items, you must use the same points of comparison in describing each. Write the names of three comparable points for each of the topics of comparison in bold.

EXAMPLE: Traditional **marriages** and modern **marriages**
a) the roles of the sexes
b) the influence of the extended family in the couple's married life
c) the husband and wife's participation in life outside the marriage

1. Online **dating** and speed **dating**
   a) _____
   b) _____
   c) _____

2. Arranged **marriages** and love **marriages**
   a) _____
   b) _____
   c) _____

3. Successful **dates** and disastrous **dates**
   a) _____
   b) _____
   c) _____

4. Long-distance **relationships** and close-proximity* **relationships**
   a) _____
   b) _____
   c) _____
   *relationships where the partners live in the same location

5. **Marriage** with children and **marriage** without children
   a) _____
   b) _____
   c) _____

6. A Greek **wedding** and an Indian **wedding**
   a) _____
   b) _____
   c) _____

7. A Dating **relationship** and a marriage **relationship**
   a) _____
   b) _____
   c) _____

8. A successful **marriage** and an unsuccessful **marriage**
   a) _____
   b) _____
   c) _____

9. **Families** with a single child and **families** with many children
   a) _____
   b) _____
   c) _____

10. **Marriages** with one husband and one wife and **marriages** with one husband and many wives

   a) _____
   b) _____
   c) _____

Exercise B

The following is a list of features comparing the family life of two different families. Read the lists of features and name the point of comparison. The first two have been done for you.

	The L Family	The M Family
1.	**Marriage**	
	couple had arranged marriage	couple had a love marriage
	couple met through family members	couple met at university
	wife married at 18, husband married at 26	wife married at 28, husband married at 29
	couple married 27 years	couple married 17 years
2.	**Career**	
	husband works as an engineer	husband works in business
	wife is a stay-at-home mother	wife works as a lawyer
3.		
	one son, two daughters	one son, one daughter
	son is 26, daughter is 24, daughter is 21	son is 12, daughter is 15
	son is engineer, daughter is a teacher, daughter is a university student	son is middle-school student, daughter is a high-school student
	son is engaged to be married	
4.		
	maternal grandparents live with the family	maternal grandparents live in Vancouver
	paternal grandparents live abroad	paternal grandparents live nearby
	four uncles and aunts live nearby	one aunt lives nearby
	six aunts and uncles live abroad	one aunt and uncle live in Vancouver
5.		
	husband: building model trains, home renovations	husband: playing hockey, investment club, ski club
	wife: book club, cooking, sewing, volunteer at newcomer-welcome centre	wife: swimming, volunteer at homeless shelter, book and ski clubs
		son: debate team, drums, ski club
		daughter: piano, curling, ski club
6.		
	Indian food	health food (forbid junk food)
	mother and grandmother cook every day	mother and father alternate cooking most nights
		Friday is family night at a local restaurant
	family eats together every night	family eats together every night
7.		
	all family members participate in yoga, meditation, and herbal medicines	all family members take a multiple vitamin daily
		family active in sports
	visit a doctor as needed	all family members visit a doctor once a year for a check-up and as needed
8.		
	Hindu-puja ritual every morning	
	daily prayer	do not pray daily
	attend temple regularly	attend church on a special occasions

Exercise C

The sentences below express similarities and differences. In each sentence, circle the joining word(s) that show comparison or contrast. Highlight any punctuation that is used with the expression.

1. Both long-distance relationships and close-proximity relationships require good communication for their success.
2. Couples in close-proximity relationships share both their positive and negative emotions. In contrast, in long-distance relationships partners often share only their positive feelings.
3. Partners who see each other face to face can easily give each other lots of hugs and kisses, but partners in long-distance relationships can't do that.
4. Long-distance relationships are different from close-proximity relationships in important ways.
5. Unlike people in face-to-face relationships, people in long-distance relationships often overlook their partner's negative personality traits.
6. Just as people in face-to-face relationships should say "I love you" often, people in long-distance relationships should also do this.
7. On the one hand, seeing each other all the time can lead to more fights. On the other hand, it can lead to more intimacy.
8. Partners in long-distance relationships miss each other if they don't talk often. Similarly, people in close-proximity relationships miss each other if they don't see each other for a while.
9. It takes planning to meet with your partner face to face. It likewise takes planning to meet with your partner online.
10. Getting to know your partner physically is easy in face-to-face relationships whereas in long-distance relationships this is hard.

> The words used to signal comparison and contrast can be coordinating conjunctions, subordinating conjunctions, or conjunctive adverbs. Depending on the placement of these words and their function, they require different punctuation. See Appendix, pages 136–37 for an explanation.

Comparison Word(s)	Contrast Word(s)
both ... and,	but
just as ... also	whereas, while, although, unlike
similarly, likewise	in contrast, on the one hand/ on the other hand
	is/are different from, differ(s) from

Exercise D

Read the list of features comparing two different families in Exercise B. Write six sentences that contrast the two families and four sentences that compare them. Use the expressions in the chart above.

Exercise E

Block-method Comparison

One way to organize information in a comparison-and-contrast paragraph is to first write about all the comparative points for one topic and then to write about the same comparative points for the second topic. This is called the block method, or *all about one and then all about the other*. The sample paragraph on pages 77–78 in this unit is written using the block method.

Point-by-point Comparison

Another way to organize a comparison-and-contrast paragraph is to make point-by-point comparisons. In this type of organization, you write about each comparative point from both perspectives before moving on to the next comparison point. This type of organization is useful when organizing complex topics. Points are clearly made because the reader is able to see the similarities and differences immediately. The sample paragraph on pages 12–13 (from the Ancient Secrets unit) in this workbook is written in the point-by-point style.

1. Read the paragraph on pages 77–78 and reorganize the information to write a point-by-point comparison. You may need to change, add, or delete a few sentences.
2. Read the paragraph on pages 12–13 and reorganize the information to write a block-method comparison. You may need to change, add, or delete a few sentences.

Exercise F

The topic sentence for a comparison-and-contrast essay indicates what is being compared or contrasted. The following patterns can be used for topic sentences.

- There are several (similarities / differences) between X and Y.
- X and Y are (similar / different) in many ways.
- X and Y have several things in common.
- A comparison between X and Y shows that ...

Write a topic sentence for the ten comparison topics in Exercise A.

Exercise G

The following sentence patterns can be used to link points of comparison and contrast.

Comparison

a) Both X and Y + verb ...
b) X and Y are similar in that + (*noun [phrase] / pronoun referring to X and Y*) + verb ...
c) X is/are similar to Y in that (*noun [phrase] / pronoun referring to X*) + verb ...
d) X + verb. Likewise, Y + verb ...
e) X + verb. Y also + verb ...
f) Like X, Y + verb ...

Contrast

g) Unlike X, Y + verb ...
h) X+ verb, but Y + verb ...
i) X + verb whereas Y + verb ...
j) X differ/differs from Y in that (*noun [phrase] / pronoun referring to X*) + verb ...
k) X is/are different from Y in that (*noun [phrase] / pronoun referring to X*) + verb ...
l) While X + verb, Y + verb ...
m) X + verb. Y, on the other hand, + verb ...

Paraphrase the sentences of comparison and contrast, using the sentence patterns indicated by the letters in parentheses.

1. In arranged marriages the families decide who is a suitable partner for the child. This is not the case in love marriages. (j)
2. Speed dating is safe because you are not alone with the person. This is also true for group dating. (a)
3. Eastern traditions value the union of whole families. Western traditions value romantic love between two individuals. (i)
4. In same-culture marriages, couples want their children to know their heritage. This is also true of couples in intercultural marriages. (e)
5. In traditional marriages, couples want the marriage to last. This is also true of couples in modern marriages. (d)
6. Eastern parents and Western parents love their children deeply and want them to succeed. (f)
7. Long-distance relationships can last a long time. Face-to-face relationships have a better chance to succeed. (h)
8. Long-distance relationships are different from face-to-face relationships. The partners can't express their feelings to each other physically. (k)
9. Men want to find suitable partners. Women are similar. (c)
10. In face-to-face communication it's easy to show how you feel about someone. In online communication, it's difficult to show how you feel about someone. (g)

Exercise H

Write a comparison-and-contrast paragraph.

- Select one of the comparison topics in Exercise A.
- List several features for each point of comparison.
- Decide whether you will use the point-by-point or block-comparison method of organization
- Use the checklist to write a paragraph.

✓ Comparison-and-Contrast Paragraph Checklist

Content

☐ Does my topic sentence state what my paragraph is about?

☐ Is it clear that my purpose is to explain, to persuade, or to inform?

☐ Do I use the most significant comparative and contrasting points to support the point of view in my topic sentence?

- [ ] Do I use the same comparative and contrastive points for each item?
- [ ] Do all my statements connect to my perspective on the topic?
- [ ] Does my concluding sentence draw the reader's attention to the topic sentence again?

Organization
- [ ] Is the information in the paragraph organized in either a point-by-point or block method?

Meaning
- [ ] Have I used appropriate words to show similarities and differences?
- [ ] Have I used precise words to communicate my meaning?

Mechanics
- [ ] Have I checked my paragraph for mistakes in grammar, spelling, and punctuation?

Academic Word List

approach	consult	normal
appropriate	involve	partners
attitude	mentality	
challenge	methods	

Word Meaning
Exercise A

Read the situation which helps to explain the meaning of the bolded word. Then choose the correct definition for the bolded word.

1. In Canada, it's **normal** for high-school students to date. Most high-school students have some dating experience by the time they graduate.

    normal (adj)
    a) typical, usual, and what you would expect
    b) healthy, good, and what you think is positive
    c) strange, curious, and what you would avoid

2. Long-distance relationships must be managed differently than close-proximity relationships because it's harder to keep a relationship going when the partners are not together very much. Couples must **approach** a long-distance relationship with more trust because they can't see whether their partner is faithful or not.

    to **approach** (v) a problem or task
    a) to avoid it
    b) to prevent it from becoming a problem
    c) to start dealing with it in a particular way

3. In some countries, dating implies a commitment to marriage in the future. In Canada and the United States, **attitudes** toward dating are very casual. Young people think dating is just a fun thing to do.

    attitudes (n) toward / about something
    a) thoughts and feelings about something
    b) worries and fears that result from bad experiences
    c) love and respect that you show toward something

4. It is common for young people to **challenge** their parents' ideas about dating and marriage. They often think their parents' views are old-fashioned.

    to **challenge** (v) something or someone
    a) to understand something well
    b) to make statements or act in ways that show you are not in agreement with someone's ideas or actions
    c) to improve something

5. Before Tracy agreed to marry Josh, she **consulted** her parents to hear what they thought.

    to **consult** (v) someone or something
    a) to seek information to help you make a decision
    b) to agree with someone's opinion about something
    c) to make a decision without thinking about it first

6. Even though Felicity's parents thought her boyfriend was an honourable man, they didn't think he would be an **appropriate** husband for her. His family was poor and her family was rich. They thought this difference would cause problems in the marriage.

    appropriate (adj)
    a) suitable, acceptable, or correct for the particular situation
    b) not good in a particular situation
    c) prepared for a particular situation

7. Building a successful marriage **involves** being flexible, patient, and trusting.

   to **involve** (v) something

   a) prevents a person from doing a particular thing
   b) leads to a particular result
   c) includes as a part

8. Velma's grandparents couldn't understand why she didn't want to get married. Their generation had a very different **mentality** when it came to expectations of women. They thought that a woman was not successful unless she was a wife and mother.

   mentality (n)

   a) a particular attitude or way of thinking of a person or a group
   b) a psychological illness
   c) a change in personality

9. Same-sex marriages are legal in Canada. We should no longer assume that marriage is between **partners** of the opposite sex.

   partners* (n)

   a) people who don't like each other or are trying to hurt each other
   b) people who are married to each other or are having a romantic relationship
   c) people who like going to parties or are outgoing

   * can also mean *a person with whom you are doing an activity*. In this meaning, no romantic relationship is implied

10. Couples can use several **methods** to reduce the risk of an unwanted pregnancy, including abstinence, taking the birth control pill, and using condoms. The only certain way to avoid a pregnancy though is to not have sex.

    methods (n)

    a) particular ways of doing something
    b) advice about how to do something
    c) general ideas about something

Pronunciation
Exercise B

Listen to your teacher or an audio dictionary to hear the pronunciation of each word in the list. Repeat each word aloud. Mark the syllables and major word stress.

1. approach (v)   ap / **proach**
2. appropriate (adj)   _____
3. attitude (n)   _____
4. challenge (v)   _____
5. consult (v)   _____
6. involve (v)   _____
7. mentality (n)   _____
8. method (n)   _____
9. normal (adj)   _____
10. partner (n)   _____

Word Forms
Exercise C

Fill in the blank with the word form shown in parentheses. Select only word forms that have the same meaning as in Exercise A.

1. approach (v): _____ (n)
2. appropriate (adj): _____ (n)
   _____ (adv)
3. attitude (n)
4. challenge (v): _____ (n)
   _____ (n)
   _____ (adj)
5. consult (v): _____ (n)
   _____ (n)
   _____ (adj)
6. involve (v): _____ (n)
   _____ (adj)
7. mentality (n): _____ (adj)
   _____ (adv)
8. method (n): _____ (n)
   _____ (adj)
   _____ (adv)
9. normal (adj): _____ (n)
   _____ (adv)
10. partner (n): _____ (n)
    _____ (v)

Exercise D

In a dictionary, find one example sentence for each word in Exercise A and copy it into your notebook. Write a second sentence of your own. Then, work with a partner to revise and edit your sentences.

Exercise E

Read the story and complete each blank with a word from the list. Use each word only once.

approach	challenging	mentality	partners
appropriate	consulted	methods	
attitudes	involve	normal	

Our ₁ _____ toward interracial dating and marriage are beginning to change as more immigrants come to Canada and more Canadians live or work abroad. In the past, most people thought it was not ₂ _____ for people of different races to date or marry. Today, interracial unions represent a strong and growing part of Canadian society. Mixed-race unions are not that ₃ _____ yet. They still make up only a small percentage (about four percent) of all marriages and common-law relationships in Canada; however, nearly 300,000 Canadians were involved in mixed marriages or mixed common-law relationships in 2006. Statistics Canada is the government agency that uses a variety of research ₄ _____ to collect information about Canadian society. It reports that this is an increase of nearly 30 percent since 2001. This trend shows a change in people's ₅ _____ regarding what is acceptable in love and marriage. Young people are ₆ _____ the belief that romantic ₇ _____ must be of the same race, religion, or culture. Their ₈ _____ to selecting a partner is changing. About 85 percent of all mixed unions ₉ _____ relationships in which one partner is white and the other is not. Canadians of Japanese descent are more likely than other visible minorities to be in a mixed relationship. People of Latin American descent are the second-most likely to be in a mixed union, followed by people who are black. Visible minorities of South Asian or Chinese origin are least likely to be involved in a mixed union. We ₁₀ _____ one expert who points out that when we think about mixed unions, most of us still think about white and black or white and Japanese. According to the expert, this is going to change. In the very near future, mixed race relationships are going to be between two visible minority groups. As the number of visible minorities in Canada continues to climb, experts agree that an increasing number of them will marry outside their ethnic group.

Unit 9
Get Those Creative Juices Flowing!

Vocabulary

Exercise A

Read the dictionary definition. Write the correct word from the list on the line. Use the symbols and abbreviations included in each word entry to help you.

associate	come	improve	passionate
attention	connect	lead	reflect
aware	focus	open	think

EXAMPLE: 1. **con·nect**
verb ~ (sb / sth <u>to</u> sb / sth) to see how people, things, events, etc. are involved with each other

Symbols and Abbreviations used in the dictionary
- *adj* — adjective
- *sb* — somebody
- *sth* — something
- IDM — idiom
- ~ — replaces the headword in the entry
- PHR V — phrasal verb
- · in headword (**con·nect**), shows where a word can be broken

2. _____
verb ~ sb / sth (<u>with</u> sb / sth) to relate two people or things in your mind

3. _____
adj (be) ~ (<u>about</u> sb /sth) having strong feelings of enthusiasm for sth

4. _____
adj (be) ~ (<u>to</u> sth) (of a person) willing to think about ideas that are new or different from your own

5. _____
verb ~ (<u>on</u> sb / sth) to give your attention, effort, etc. to a specific subject, situation, or person

6. _____
adj [not before noun] (be) ~ (<u>of</u> sth) knowing or realizing sth

7. _____
IDM *verb* ~ (<u>up with</u> sth) [no passive] to find or suggest an idea, etc.

8. _____
verb (pay) ~ (<u>to</u> sb / sth) listen to or watch sth / sb carefully

9. _____
PHR V (<u>on</u> sth) to create sth that is better than what was before it

10. _____
verb ~ (<u>to</u> sth) to bring sb or sth to a particular result

11. _____
verb ~ (<u>on</u> sth) to think carefully about sth

12. _____
verb ~ (<u>about</u> sth) to consider an idea or problem

Exercise B

The following example sentences were left out from the dictionary entries in Exercise A. Use the words in Exercise A to fill in the blanks with the correct phrases.

1. Copying other people's work _____ **to** conformity.

2. He **was** _____ **of** the risks of not following the rules.

3. History helps us to understand the world better because it _____ the present **to** the past.

4. I always _____ the smell of baking **with** my childhood.

5. I can't give you an answer now. I'll have to _____ **about** it first.

6. Isaac Newton **was** _____ **about** physics, astronomy, and mathematics.

7. Photographers have to **pay** _____ **to** the light in order to take good pictures.

8. She _____ up with a new idea for increasing sales.

9. She wanted to _____ on the implications of her decision.

10. The business meeting _____ on three main problems.

11. The company _____ on its cellphone last year by adding a GPS to the new design.

12. The teacher **was** _____ **to** suggestions by her students about what she should teach them in English class.

Grammar Focus

Information questions
Exercise A

Put the sentence parts in the right order to make an information question.

1. [?] [Shakespeare] [When did] [live]
   _____

2. [?] [Leonard Cohen] [live] [Where did] [as a child]
   _____

3. [?] [lose their creativity] [Why do children] [as they get older]
   _____

4. [?] [How] [help their children] [can parents] [to be creative]
   _____

5. [?] [company] [today] [the most innovative] [What is]
   _____

6. [?] [encourage] [creativity] [What classroom activities]
   _____

7. [?] [Why is] [so important] [innovation]
   _____

8. [?] [the most famous poet] [in your home country] [Who is]
   _____

9. [?] [you are creating] [How do you feel when] [something new]
   _____

10. [?] [What techniques] [new ideas] [do you use] [to generate]
    _____

Exercise B

Read the information about this famous person in recent history (1915–2009). Ask the questions that would give you the information.

1. Les Paul
   Who _____?

2. He is famous for inventing the solid-body electric guitar in 1952.
   a) Why _____?
   b) What _____?

3. He was an American guitarist, songwriter, and inventor.
   What _____?

4. He began to play his first musical instrument, the harmonica, at the age of eight.
   a) When _____?
   b) What _____?

5. He was born June 9, 1915, and died August 12, 2009, of pneumonia in White Plains, New York.
   a) When _____?
   b) Where _____?
   c) How _____?

6. He recorded 40 albums during his lifetime.
   How _____?

Exercise C

Choose a famous creative person alive today or in recent history from your home culture. Use the Internet to get some information about this person. Create an activity like the one in Exercise B. Be prepared to exchange it with another classmate.

Exercise D

One hundred people were surveyed about creativity and the arts. Below are some of the survey results. What *wh-* question do you think the researcher asked to get this information? Use as many different question words as you can.

EXAMPLE: Top three results for movie preferences:

action films / romance movies / science-fiction films

Survey Question: <u>What kind of movies do you like?</u>

1. Top <u>three</u> music preferences:

    pop music / hip hop / jazz

    Survey Question: _____

2. <u>Three</u> most popular fantasy movies:

    Lord of the Rings: The Fellowship of the Ring / Harry Potter and the Philosopher's Stone / Edward Scissorhands

    Survey Question: _____

3. Top time of day for being most creative:

    late at night

    Survey Question: _____

4. <u>Three</u> most popular reading genres:

    romance novels / mystery novels / action thrillers

    Survey Question: _____

5. <u>Three</u> best male actors in this decade:

    Brad Pitt / Tom Hanks / Leonardo Di Caprio

    Survey Question: _____

6. Top <u>three</u> places for fashion designers to work:

    New York, United States / Hong Kong, China / Milan, Italy

    Survey Question: _____

7. Top <u>two</u> reasons children become less creative as they get older

    because they have to follow too many rules in school / because jobs in the arts pay less than jobs in business and science

    Survey Question: _____

8. Top <u>three</u> ways people stay creative

    play / be curious / think outside the box

    Survey Question: _____

Exercise E

Read one blogger's response to the question, "What is the most famous anime?" Use the prompt to write out the full *wh-* question that will give you the information in **bold**.

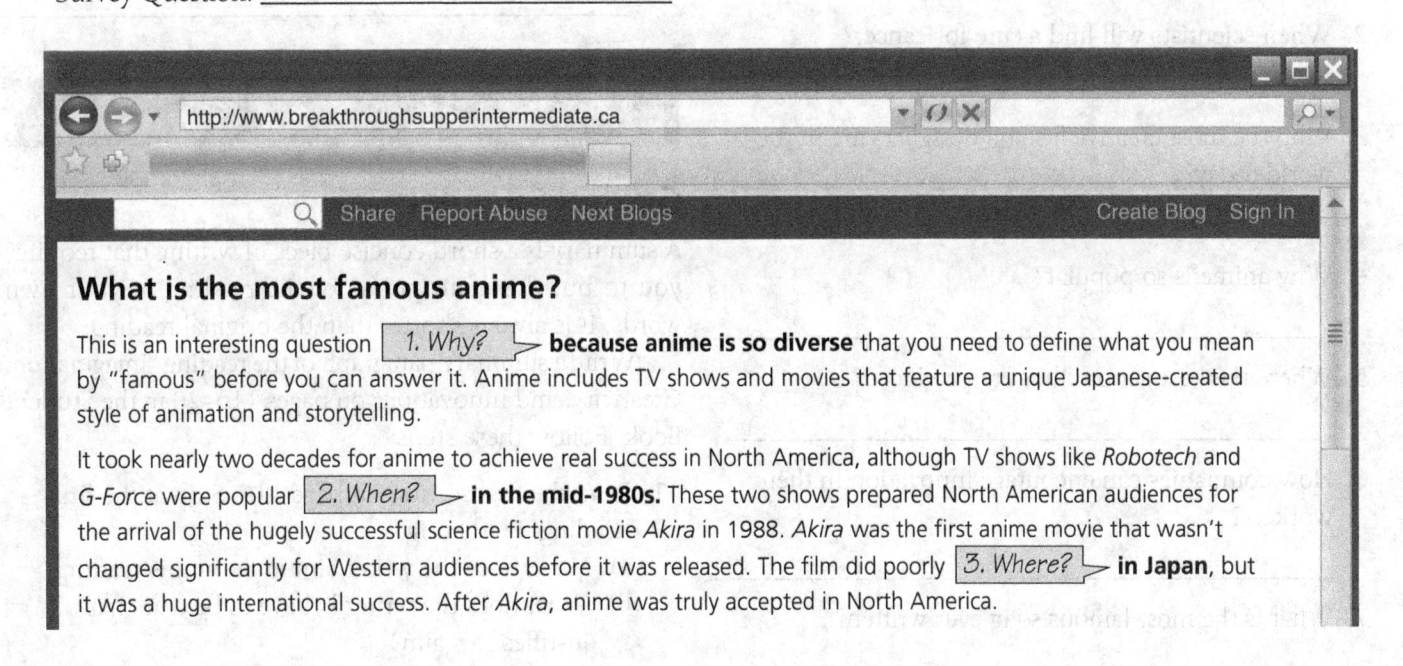

---

http://www.breakthroughsupperintermediate.ca

What is the most famous anime?

This is an interesting question [1. Why?] **because anime is so diverse** that you need to define what you mean by "famous" before you can answer it. Anime includes TV shows and movies that feature a unique Japanese-created style of animation and storytelling.

It took nearly two decades for anime to achieve real success in North America, although TV shows like *Robotech* and *G-Force* were popular [2. When?] **in the mid-1980s**. These two shows prepared North American audiences for the arrival of the hugely successful science fiction movie *Akira* in 1988. *Akira* was the first anime movie that wasn't changed significantly for Western audiences before it was released. The film did poorly [3. Where?] **in Japan**, but it was a huge international success. After *Akira*, anime was truly accepted in North America.

Classic anime films like *Laputa: Castle in the Sky* and *My Neighbor Totoro* combined [4. What?] — **detailed, colour-rich animation and classic storytelling that speaks to everyone**. They were produced in the 1980s, and they made it possible for *Spirited Away* to win the 2003 Academy Award for Best Animated Feature.

The best anime shows and movies connect with their audience by touching on emotions that—regardless of age, gender, nationality, or ethnicity—we all share. [5. Who?] — **Hayao Miyazaki** is the most famous director of anime. He is responsible for countless classic movies, including *Kiki's Delivery Service*, *Princess Mononoke*, and *Howl's Moving Castle*.

There have been a number of changes to the anime genre [6. Why?] — **because computer technology and animation have improved over the last decade**. Series like *Ghost in the Shell*, *Appleseed*, and *Final Fantasy* have incorporated a new digital style of art that adds more detail to their futuristic technology, and makes the characters appear even more human.

Anime is now firmly established in Western culture with shows like *Pokémon* and *Bleach*. Today it has become even harder to tell if a production was Japanese-made, like *Afro Samurai*, or an American-created franchise, like *Avatar: The Last Airbender*. [7. How many?] — **More than 650** episodes of *Pokémon* have aired on television, and the video-game inspired program shows no signs of stopping!

For me, the most famous anime isn't decided by the money it has generated or the number of episodes that have been aired. I think *Robotech* is the most famous anime [8. Why?] — **because it played such an important role in my youth**. When I was young, I used to race home every day to see the show at 4:00 p.m.—I never missed an episode. *Robotech* will always be one of my fondest childhood memories, and therefore, the most famous anime for me. Which is your most famous anime?

Grammar Edit

Six of the questions below have errors and four are correct. Mark C if the question is correct. Mark E if the question has an error, and correct it.

1. What colour of carpet will fit with a brown leather sofa?

   _____

2. When scientists will find a cure for cancer?

   _____

3. Who the most creative fashion designers are in the world today?

   _____

4. Why anime is so popular?

   _____

5. Where the best action films are produced?

   _____

6. How companies can encourage innovation in their workers?

   _____

7. What is the most famous song ever written?

8. What will be the next great scientific discovery?

   _____

9. Who composed the famous ballet Swan Lake?

   _____

10. Where you will find the magnificent ceramics of Persepolis?

    _____

Reading

Guided Summary

A summary is a short, concise piece of writing that requires you to put the main points of the reading in your own words. It is always shorter than the original reading.

Write a summary paragraph of the reading "Imagination, Creativity, and Innovation" on pages 116–20 in the Student Book. Follow these steps:

1. Read the first section on page 116. Stop at the first heading, Predicting.
   a) What does the writer aim to do in this reading?
   b) What does the writer believe to be true that justifies this aim?

2. Read each of the seven headings that describe a principle of creativity. Explain each principle in one or two sentences.

Writing

Model Paragraph

I'm a songwriter, but writing a new song is not always easy. A few years ago I wrote a song called "Trees Running Backwards." It's one of my best songs. The idea came to me while I was travelling from Nova
5 Scotia to Ontario by train. I was raised in Ontario, but I was living in Nova Scotia at the time. I was travelling by train to Ontario to celebrate Thanksgiving with my folks. At first the ride was just like any other ride. First, I read the newspaper. Then, I watched a movie
10 on my laptop. After that, I listened to music to pass the time. As the train pulled into Montreal, I saw an attractive young woman waiting to board the train. She walked into my train car when the door opened. The attraction was instant and crushing. My heart
15 began to beat faster as she moved down the aisle to claim the seat next to me. After she had settled in, she looked my way and our eyes locked. "Trees running backwards," she said with a smile. "Excuse me?" I said. I had no idea what she was talking about. "I love
20 travelling by train," she explained, "the steady rhythm of wheels moving over tracks, trees flying by as the train races through the countryside. It's like the trees are running backwards." I nodded appreciatively. We didn't say much after that, but for the rest of the trip I
25 thought about what she had said. I felt the beat of the train rushing over the tracks and soaked in the sight of the trees ... running backwards. The train arrived in Toronto at 8:10 p.m. Before heading to my parent's house, I stopped in at a small, nearly empty coffee
30 shop. I grabbed a pen and paper and quickly wrote down the song that was playing in my head. At last, after months of struggling to find a new song, the song found me.

1. What is the writer's aim in this paragraph?
2. Who is the story about? When did it happen? Where did it happen? What happened in the story?
3. How is the information in the story organized?
4. What transitional expressions are used to signal the order of events?
5. Is there any information in the story that does not support the main idea?

> **Narrative Paragraphs**
>
> The narrative paragraph tells a story, which explains something. It makes the reader feel involved in the story or have an emotional reaction to it. It describes important details such as who is involved, where the story takes place, when, why and how it happens. An effective narrative paragraph is ordered chronologically.

Exercise A

Put the following sentences in chronological order so the story makes sense. Write the order number on the line at the beginning of the sentence.

_1_ a) Once there was a little boy who wanted his dad to teach him how to play catch. One sunny morning the little boy's father was sitting on the couch, drinking a beer, while watching a baseball game. The little boy was playing outside.

___ b) "It was simple," stated the boy. "On the back of the world was a picture of a person, and once I put the person together that's when their world came together too."

___ c) A few moments later the boy returned and said, "I put the world together, Daddy. Can we play catch now?"

___ d) After a few moments of tearing the magazine cover, the father placed the torn pieces on top of the magazine.

___ e) During the 10 minutes that his son was gone, the father had opened another cold beer and another inning had started. Frustrated by the boy's third interruption, the dad looked around the room.

___ f) Five minutes later the boy returned screaming, "Daddy, let's play some catch now!"

___ g) Hesitatingly, the boy took the magazine and went to his room as he cried, "Okay, Daddy, I won't."

___ h) Surprised, the father looked at his son, and there in his small hands was the magazine with the world pieced perfectly together. Amazed, the dad asked his child how he put the world together so quickly.

___ i) Ten minutes later the boy returned with a ball and glove in his hand. He was waiting for his father to play some catch. "Daddy, let's go. I want to be a famous baseball player," shouted the boy.

___ j) The boy rushed into the house shouting, "Daddy, Daddy, Daddy, show me how to play catch!"

___ k) The father turned to the boy and said, "Is five minutes up already? Just wait a little longer, Son. The inning is not quite over yet. Come back in ten more minutes."

___ l) Ten more minutes?" whined the son. "Okay," he said and shuffled out of the room.

___ m) The father, who was staring at the television screen, replied, "I can't play catch right now. We'll play in a little while, Son. Let me finish watching this inning. Come back in five minutes."

___ n) Then, the father turned to his boy and said "Son, once you put this picture of the world back together we can play catch, but do not interrupt me again until you are done!"

___ o) While scanning the room the father noticed a magazine underneath the coffee table. On the cover of the magazine was a large detailed picture of the world. The father wanted to give the boy something to do, so he began tearing the magazine cover into small pieces like a puzzle.

For a story to be effective, it has to move smoothly from one action to another. Writers use tenses to show the sequence of actions. They also use words such as the following to signal time order and to indicate when one action finishes and another action begins.

- first … at first …
- then …
- next … the next *day* (*morning / afternoon / evening / night*) …
- later … a little while later
- before
- after … after a while
- when … that *day* (*morning / afternoon / evening / night*) … at that time
- as soon as
- while … as …
- now … today … this *morning* (*evening / week / month / year*)
- yesterday … last *night* (*week / month / year*)
- tomorrow … the next *day* (*morning / evening / week / month / year*)
- finally

Exercise B

Replace the bolded time phrases in each sentence with a time expression from the list. More than one answer may be possible.

at first	a little while later
after a while	finally
as soon as	first
as	

1. (a) (**In the beginning**) _____ she really liked the large modern art sculpture in her living room. (b) (**Some time later**) _____ she got bored with it.

2. The audience was a little bored with the opening band at the music concert. (**The moment when**) _____ the main band arrived on stage, the fans screamed and applauded.

3. (a) (**In the beginning**), _____ the actor seemed a bit nervous, but (b) (**during the time when**) _____ the first act ended, he relaxed and began to give a great performance.

4. (a) (**Before all other things**), _____ the acrobat juggled three fireballs in the air. (b) (**A short time after that**), _____

he added three sharp knives. (c) (**In the end**), _____ he juggled the fireballs, the knives, and three sheets of glass at the same time.

5. (**The moment when**) _____ the violinist finished her magnificent performance, the audience rose to its feet for a standing ovation.

6. (**During the time when**) _____ the lights came up on the stage, the fans roared in anticipation of their favourite rock star.

Exercise C

Read the two paragraphs that tell the story about a lesson in art. Fill in each blank with a time expression from the list that shows an appropriate time relationship. Use each time expression only once.

after	last month	that night
after a while	now	the next morning
at first	that afternoon	when

Brian Bristles was an artistic boy. He saw a beautiful painting in everything and, in the blink of an eye, he could paint anything at all, filling it with magic and colour. 1_____, Brian and his grandfather spent a weekend at the home of a famous chess player, Martin Maxim. Mr. Maxim was an old friend of Brian's grandfather. 2_____ they arrived, Brian went into a large room and found a lovely hand-carved chess set with a black-and-white marble chess board. The chess set caught Brian's artistic eye. 3_____, he thought it was beautiful, but 4_____ he felt that the chess pieces looked too much alike. The black-and-white chess pieces and the black-and-white marble board made the set look boring. So, 5_____ after everyone was asleep, Brian took his paint box and painted each chess piece in the most colourful way, so that no two pieces looked alike. 6_____ he had painted all the chess pieces, he painted a beautiful scene on the marble chessboard. Brian hoped his art would please his grandfather and Mr. Maxim. 7_____ after breakfast, Mr. Maxim discovered that his pieces had been covered in a thousand different colours, but instead of being pleased, he was very angry. He had a very important match to play 8_____ at three o'clock. All the different coloured chess pieces were beautiful, but 9_____ it was impossible to play chess because the players couldn't tell which pieces belonged to them. The squares of the board were covered with a painting, so the players couldn't see the squares. It was impossible for the players to see where to move their chess pieces. Brian's grandfather explained to him that even the loveliest, most colourful things need to have some order to them. Brian's feelings were hurt, but he was a true artist, and he wasn't going to give up easily.

a little while later	before	finally
when	now	

10 _____ Brian went to his grandfather and Mr. Maxim and asked their permission to fix what he had done. They knew that the artistic boy was clever, so they decided to give him a chance. Brian went off and spent hours alone with his paints. 11_____ he was finished, shortly 12_____ the match was about to begin, he called for the two men and showed them his work. What a beautiful chess set it was! 13_____ there were two perfectly recognizable teams: that of night and that of day. On one side, the board and the pieces had been decorated with dozens of stars and moons of all sizes and colours.

On the other side, there were suns, clouds, and rainbows. The whole set had a wonderful sense of order and harmony. The two grown-ups looked at the paintings and smiled. ₁₄ _____, Brian understood that a little order had been missing from his first attempt to make the chess set more creative. He had managed to impose some order to his work without giving up any colour. It was obvious that Brian Bristles would become a great artist.

Exercise D

Read the title, first sentence and last sentence of the paragraph. Use the picture prompts to write the paragraph and tell the story. Add time words or expressions to make the sequence of events clear.

What a Wild Dream!
I had a very strange dream last night. _____

_____

_____

_____

_____

_____

_____

_____

_____

_____ I wonder what it all meant.

✔ Narrative Paragraph Checklist

Content
- ☐ Does my topic sentence tell the main point of my story?
- ☐ Have I chosen only the important events that relate to the main point of the story?
- ☐ Does my concluding sentence draw the reader's attention to the topic sentence again?

Organization
- ☐ Do I begin with one or two sentences that introduce the situation or background of the story?
- ☐ Have I organized the events in the paragraph in chronological order?

Meaning
- ☐ Have I used appropriate words or expressions to show time order?
- ☐ Have I used precise words to describe the events?
- ☐ Have I used tenses effectively to show time order?

Mechanics
- ☐ Have I checked my paragraph for mistakes in grammar, spelling, and punctuation?

Academic Word List

affect	environment	research
creativity	perspectives	rely
demonstrate	potential	
energy	principles	

Word Meaning
Exercise A

Fill in each blank with the correct word from the list above.

1. One way to _____ independent thinking is to not copy other people's ideas. This shows that you can think for yourself.

2. It is easier to solve a problem when you look at it from different _____. Different people have different ways of seeing things.

3. _____ is not just about art. It's also about thinking in new and imaginative ways.

4. People work better in offices that are painted nicely, are decorated with beautiful pictures, and have comfortable lighting. A beautiful office _____ can increase productivity.

5. We _____ on our smell to taste our food. If your sense of smell is not good, you will not enjoy the taste of the food you eat.

6. Here are some basic rules to follow for decorating a home. First, keep a similar style in each room. This creates harmony. Second, have one focal point in each room. A focal point draws attention and is interesting to look at. Finally, use some contrast. For example, if your sofa is black, use white pillows. If you follow these design _____, you will have a beautiful home.

7. The teacher's _____ is appealing. The students love his enthusiasm and excitement.

8. Everything in the world is interconnected. One thing influences another. How you treat others will _____ how they treat you.

9. Even though the student's art work still needs improvement, the teacher thinks he shows great _____. She believes that one day he will become a great artist.

10. Scientists have carefully studied what happens when people enjoy beautiful paintings, music, or sculpture. Their _____ tells us that when we appreciate art, our emotions and thinking are working together.

Pronunciation
Exercise B

Listen to your teacher or an audio dictionary to hear the pronunciation of each word in the list. Repeat each word aloud. Mark the syllables and major word stress.

1. affect (v) — af / **fěct**
2. creativity (n) _____
3. demonstrate (v) _____
4. energy (n) _____
5. environment (n) _____
6. perspective (n) _____
7. potential (n) _____
8. principle (n) _____
9. research (n) _____
10. rely (v) _____

Word Forms
Exercise C

Fill in each blank with the word form shown in parentheses. Select only word forms that have the same meaning as in Exercise A.

1. affect (v)
2. creativity (n): _____ (v)
   _____ (adj)
   _____ (adv)
3. demonstrate (v): _____ (n)
   _____ (n)
   _____ (adj)
   _____ (adj)
   _____ (adv)
4. energy (n): _____ (v)
   _____ (adj)
   _____ (adv)
5. environment (n): _____ (adj)
   _____ (adv)

6. perspective (n) _____
7. potential (n): _____ (adj)
   _____ (adv)
8. principle (n): _____ (adj)
9. research (n): _____ (n)
   _____ (v)
10. rely (v): _____ (n)
    _____ (adj)
    _____ (adv)

Exercise D

In a dictionary, find one example sentence for each word in Exercise A and copy it into your notebook. Write a second sentence of your own. Then, work with a partner to revise and edit your sentences.

Exercise E

Read the following paragraph and complete each blank with a word from the list. Use each word only once.

affect	environment	research
creative	perspectives	rely
demonstrated	potential	
energy	principles	

It is not uncommon for people to have times during their lives when they become depressed. Some symptoms of depression include feeling sad, losing interest in daily activities, sleeping too much or not enough, low ₁_____ and feelings of worthlessness or guilt. These symptoms often go away after a short while, but sometimes they last longer. People think that they must take medication to treat depression. Sometimes medication is necessary, but there are other ₂_____ ways to treat depression. Music therapy, pet therapy, yoga, meditation, and acupuncture can all help to manage depression. Did you know that diet and the ₃_____ can ₄_____ a person's mood? One Spanish ₅_____ study ₆_____ a connection between junk food and the risk of depression. Factors in a person's social and physical environment such as stress from a relationship break-up, or lack of light can also lead to depression. Changing your lifestyle has the ₇_____ to reduce the risk and symptoms of depression, so that people suffering from depression do not have to ₈_____ on drugs, which can have negative side effects, to treat the illness. Of course, doctors and social workers may have different ₉_____ on how to treat depression, but they agree on these ₁₀_____ for reducing the risk of depression: eat a healthy diet, exercise, and build an active social network of friends and family. If you think you may be suffering from depression, seek the advice of your doctor before starting any treatment.

Unit 10
That's So Canadian

Vocabulary

Exercise A
Label each picture with a word from the list to show its meaning. Use each word only once.

anglophone	identity	multicultural
custom	image	prime minister
First Nations	Inuit	stereotype
francophone	lifestyle	symbol
heritage	Mountie	

a) _____

b) _____

c) _____

d) person from the _____

e) _____

f) _____

g) _____

h) _____

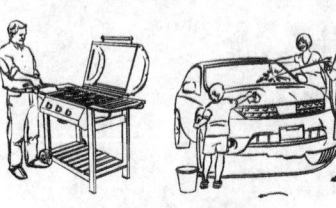

i) _____

j) _____

k) _____

l) _____

m) _____

Sir John A. Macdonald,
first leader of Canada

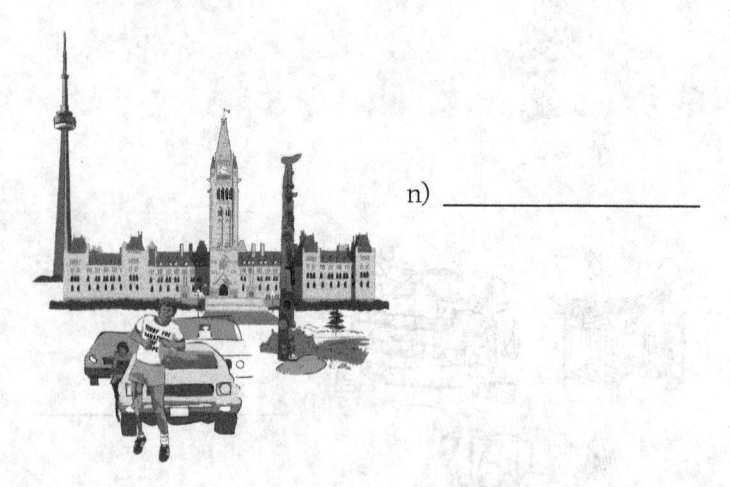

n) _____

Exercise B

Write a word from the list in Exercise A to complete the sentences.

1. A national flag is a _____ of pride for nations around the world.

2. British Columbia is an _____ province. There are few French speakers there.

3. Halloween is a great day to wear a costume like the uniform of a member of Canada's national police force. A _____ wears a traditional red coat, black pants, brown leather boots, and a tan hat.

4. In Canada, it is the _____ to shake someone's hand when you first meet them.

5. Quebec is a _____ province. French is the official language.

6. Stephen Harper was _____ of Canada in 2011.

7. The _____ people were the first settlers of the land that later became Canada.

8. The _____ of Canada's north have lived there for thousands of years.

9. The _____ of the Mountie that most people have is of someone who is tall, strong, and courageous.

10. The railroad system that connects the east and west coasts is an important part of Canadian _____.

11. Welcoming immigrants, peace keeping, and being polite are all important parts of the Canadian _____. Canadians feel these characteristics make them unique.

12. In a _____ society with people of different beliefs and customs, creativity and innovation grow.

13. Participating in outdoor activities is an important part of the Canadian _____ because Canadians enjoy the beauty of the seasons and the landscape.

14. The _____ of the overweight, undereducated, beer-drinking Canadian man was promoted in the 1980s by a couple of comedic characters, Bob and Doug McKenzie, but it's just not true.

Grammar Focus

Articles

Exercise A

Read the sentence. Look at the *article* and the **noun (phrase)** it qualifies. Then, check all the boxes that are true about the noun (phrase). Some sentences have no article (Ø).

1. Most Canadians want to own *a* **home**.
   - ❏ It is singular ❏ It is countable ❏ It is specified
   - ❏ It is plural ❏ It is uncountable ❏ It is unspecified

2. Most people in Canada live in *a* **city**.
   - ❏ It is singular ❏ It is countable ❏ It is specified
   - ❏ It is plural ❏ It is uncountable ❏ It is unspecified

3. *A* **driver's licence** is an acceptable form of identification in Canada.
   - ❏ It is singular ❏ It is countable ❏ It is specified
   - ❏ It is plural ❏ It is uncountable ❏ It is unspecified

4. You do not need *a* **passport** to travel between provinces.
   - ❏ It is singular ❏ It is countable ❏ It is specified
   - ❏ It is plural ❏ It is uncountable ❏ It is unspecified

5. Hockey is *the* **most popular sport** in Canada.
   - ❏ It is singular ❏ It is countable ❏ It is specified
   - ❏ It is plural ❏ It is uncountable ❏ It is unspecified

6. Canoeing and camping in *the* **Canadian wilderness** are popular pastimes.
   - ❏ It is singular ❏ It is countable ❏ It is specified
   - ❏ It is plural ❏ It is uncountable ❏ It is unspecified

7. *The* **First Nations people of Canada** are working hard to maintain their languages and cultures.
   - ❏ It is singular ❏ It is countable ❏ It is specified
   - ❏ It is plural ❏ It is uncountable ❏ It is unspecified

8. Canadians love to drink **coffee**.
   - ❏ It is singular ❏ It is countable ❏ It is specified
   - ❏ It is plural ❏ It is uncountable ❏ It is unspecified

9. It is common for **high-school students** to work part-time.
   - ❏ It is singular ❏ It is countable ❏ It is specified
   - ❏ It is plural ❏ It is uncountable ❏ It is unspecified

10. **Permanent residents** may not vote.
    - ❏ It is singular ❏ It is countable ❏ It is specified
    - ❏ It is plural ❏ It is uncountable ❏ It is unspecified

Exercise B

Read the sentences about Canada and Canadian society. Fill in the blanks with an appropriate article (*a/an*, *the*, or Ø) for the noun (phrase) in **bold**. Use the chart on page 134 and the rules on page 158 of your Student Book to help you.

1. _____ **Canadian way of living** is very informal.

2. In _____ **workplace**, dress is often casual.

3. People address each other by _____ **first names**.

4. A handshake is (a) _____ **normal form of greeting** for both (b) _____ **men** and (c) _____ **women** when people are introduced to someone new.

5. (a) _____ **Canadians** believe that your success in (b) _____ **life** should come from your own efforts and not as a favour from others.

6. Canadians believe that _____ **cheating** is shameful and wrong.

7. It is expected that people will line up and wait their turn in (a) _____ **public offices**, (b) _____ **grocery stores**, and on (c) _____ **buses**.

8. All citizens expect _____ **same opportunities** and access to services regardless of age, gender, income, occupation, race, or sexual orientation.

9. Canadians put _____ **value** on personal privacy.

10. (a) _____ **person's medical, work, or educational information** is not given to (b) _____ **family member** without (c) _____ **person's approval**.

11. Individuals have _____ **right** to see information that public and private organizations have about them.

12. _____ **divorce rate** in Canada is almost 50 percent.

13. Any property that was bought as a couple is equally distributed by law if _____ **relationship** ends.

14. _____ **Canadian parents** believe it is their job to their raise their children to live independently.

15. One fear that elderly Canadians have is that they will become dependent on their children later in _____ **life**.

Exercise C

Read the story about the camping trip. Complete each blank with *a/an*, *the*, or Ø. Use the chart on page 134 and the rules on page 158 of your Student Book to help you.

My first camping trip was with my grandparents when I was six years old.

1. My grandparents wanted me to have _____ memorable camping experience.
2. So, we tried to catch _____ rabbit to keep as a pet.
3. My grandpa put _____ box up on a forked twig, a small piece of wood that looked like a fork.
4. He tied a string to _____ twig and stuck a carrot underneath the box.
5. If an animal grabbed (a) _____ carrot, (b) _____ box would fall and trap it.
6. Then, we snuck back into our tent and waited for _____ rabbit to come.
7. Finally, we heard _____ noise! There was something in our box!
8. We pulled _____ string excitedly. We were so happy that our plan had worked.
9. Then, we crept up on (a) _____ box, gently raised (b) _____ lid, and got sprayed by (c) _____ skunk.
10. After that moment, the only thing I remember is taking a bath in _____ tomato juice and hearing my sisters make fun of me for smelling bad.
11. My grandparents were shocked that I begged them to go camping again. They were even more shocked that my parents agreed to let me go again after _____ disaster on our first trip.
12. Even though _____ first trip had had a pretty stinky ending, it was definitely memorable.

Grammar Edit

Ella did a dictation in her English class. Her teacher read a quote from someone describing how Canadians feel about their country and themselves. Ella wrote down key words and then reconstructed the paragraph. She did quite a good job although she made a few mistakes in articles. Her teacher has highlighted where the mistakes are. Help Ella to fix the mistakes. Cross out each mistake and write the noun phrase with the correct article *a/an*, *the*, or Ø above it.

I think all Canadians should have ₁ **map of Canada** in their house. It should be displayed in ₂ **place** where one can sit and think about how incredibly large and beautiful this land is. As Canadians we are continuously looking for an identity—a way to define ourselves, and a feeling of love for our country. We are still trying to describe who we are as Canadians. Many of us think that American flag-waving, hand over heart while singing out ₃ **a words** to the national anthem is too loud and enthusiastic. We admire ₄ **an American national spirit** of Americans, but Canadians are, in contrast, calmer. To understand how ₅ **the Canadians** feel in their hearts, look at our majestic landscape with its quiet, serene beauty. We are proud of this nation and of who we are. We just don't say it. It's like ₆ **a map**. It just sits there on ₇ **wall** displaying the long, gentle lines of our coasts, the power of our waterways, and the grandness of our northern territories. The vastness of our magnificent landscape takes my breath away. It brings ₈ **the tear** to my eye ... "O Canada"...

Reading

Guided Response

Oral poetry, especially in a poetry slam, is written to be performed. The impression the performance leaves on its listeners is as important as the written words. An effective oral poem creates clear images, expresses strong emotions, and evokes an emotional connect between the poem and the audience.

Read the poem, "We Are More," on pages 137–38 of the Student Book again (or listen to a performance of the poem). Use information from the following prompts to summarize your impression of the poem.

1. Who is the poet?
2. What type of poem is "We Are More"?
3. What is the purpose of this type of poetry?
4. What audience is the poet speaking to in this poem?
5. What main point is the poet is trying to make?
6. What three or four images are the most important to you personally for making this point?
7. What emotions does the poet express in the text?
8. What impression about Canada do the images and the structure leave you with?
9. Which two or three lines in the poem have the greatest effect on you?
10. What message do the last five lines of the poem emphasize?

Writing

Model Paragraph

The dictionary defines beaver as "an animal with a wide flat tail and strong teeth," but for Canadians the beaver is much more than that. Since the first explorers arrived on the shores of Canada and started
5 the fur trade, the beaver has played an important role in the country's history. European settlers traded and bought beaver furs from Aboriginal people, then manufactured coats and hats from the fur and sold these in European markets for a good profit. From
10 the 1600s to the late 1800s, the successful beaver fur trade financed a lot of Canada's development, including building its national railroad. Because of the economic importance of the beaver in Canada's history, the beaver became a popular Canadian
15 symbol at that time. Many Canadian companies such as the Hudson's Bay Company and the Canadian Pacific Railway used the hardworking beaver in their emblems. A picture of the beaver was shown on the first Canadian postage stamp in 1851. It was made an
20 official emblem of Canada on March 24, 1975. The beaver, the largest rodent in North America, can be found near rivers throughout North America. Its most prominent location today, however, is on the back of the five-cent coin. When we see the beaver symbol,
25 we think about more than just the animal; we think of the important economic role it has played in making Canada a great country.

1. What is the writer's aim in this paragraph?
2. What is the topic of the paragraph?
3. What is the topic sentence?
4. How does the writer develop the definition of the beaver?
   a) describes important characteristics of the beaver
   b) compares the beaver to another familiar symbol
   c) provides historical information about the beaver

Definition Paragraphs

A definition paragraph explains what something is. It can describe an object, an idea, a person, or other item. It usually begins by stating the general classification to which the item belongs and then describes its important qualities and features.

One reason for writing a definition paragraph is simply to extend the formal dictionary definition of an item or idea to create a clearer and more detailed description. The paragraph gives additional factual information, such as a physical description or the advantages of the item.

Another reason for writing a definition paragraph is to give the writer's interpretation (opinion) of the item or idea. In this case, the writer explains how the item or idea differs from its usual definition

Definition paragraphs include three kinds of information: 1) the word or phrase being defined, 2) the class (general group) the item or idea belongs to; and 3) its important qualities. A class is a general group of things whose individual members share similar qualities or features. For example, an *apple* belongs to the class *fruit*. A *chair* belongs to the class *furniture*.

Exercise A

For each set of objects, identify the general class. Write the class on the line.

1. canoe / kayak / ferry

   Class: _____

2. loonie / toonie / buck

   Class: _____

3. hockey / lacrosse / curling

   Class: _____

4. mountains / valleys / forests

   Class: _____

5. CBC radio / *The Globe and Mail* newspaper / CTV television

   Class: _____

6. maple leaf / beaver / Mountie

   Class: _____

7. singer-songwriter Leonard Cohen / writer W. O. Mitchell / painter Emily Carr

   Class: _____

8. Judaism / Islam / Christianity

   Class: _____

9. the Chinese are good at math / beautiful women aren't smart / all politicians are corrupt

   Class: _____

10. everyone has the right to life / no one should be a slave / no one should be tortured

    Class: _____

Exercise B

> Several patterns can be used to define an item or idea:
> X is + noun (phrase) …
> X is defined as + noun (phrase) …
> X is a kind of + noun (phrase) …
> X is called / is known as + noun (phrase) ….
> The term / word X means / refers to / signifies ….
>
> EXAMPLE: *The Canadarm is a Canadian-made mechanical device used on the Space Shuttle to move materials from one location to another outside the spacecraft.*
>
> Term: *Canadarm*
>
> Class: *mechanical device*
>
> Important feature(s): *used to move materials from one location to another outside the spacecraft.*

The following items are great Canadian inventions. First, identify the class and important features. Then, write your own definition for the word, using the expressions in the box. Finally, copy a dictionary definition for the same word.

1. zipper
   a) Class: _____
   b) Important feature(s): _____
   c) My definition: _____
   d) Dictionary definition: _____

2. insulin
   a) Class: _____
   b) Important feature(s): _____
   c) My definition: _____
   d) Dictionary definition: _____

3. snowshoes
   a) Class: _____
   b) Important feature(s): _____
   c) My definition: _____
   d) Dictionary definition: _____

4. basketball
   a) Class: _____
   b) Important feature(s): _____
   c) My definition: _____
   d) Dictionary definition: _____

5. snowmobile
   a) Class: _____
   b) Important feature(s): _____
   c) My definition: _____
   d) Dictionary definition: _____

Exercise C

There are several ways to provide details that help make a good definition.

a) Details: describe detailed physical characteristics and distinguishing features

b) Comparison: define the unfamiliar by showing its likeness to something familiar

c) Example: give a typical example

d) Negation: give a description of *what it is not* in order to clarify *what it is*

e) Origin / chronology: tell where the object or idea comes from; give historical information

f) Uses: tell how the object is used (process) or what it is used for (function)

Identify which method is being used in the following sentences that help to define the Canadian Rocky Mountains. Write the letter beside the sentence.

1. Much of the mountain range is used by tourists for camping, hiking, and skiing. _____

2. The Rocky Mountains are a major mountain range in western North America. _____

3. The Rocky Mountains were formed over 55 million years ago when tectonic plates in the earth moved significantly. _____

4. The Rocky Mountains are not the same as the Pacific Coast Mountain Ranges, which are located directly on the Pacific Coast. _____

5. Mount Robson in British Columbia is the highest peak in the Canadian Rockies. _____

6. The Rocky Mountains are an important habitat for many animals such as moose, white-tailed deer, mountain goats, bighorn sheep, black bears, grizzly bears, coyotes, lynxes, and wolverines. _____

7. The Rocky Mountains are not as high as the Swiss Alps. _____

Exercise D

Include examples when defining something that may be unfamiliar to the reader. Introduce examples with expressions like *an example of this is ...*, *for example ...*, *for instance ...*, or *such as ...* Provide two examples for each general statement below.

1. The maple leaf is an important Canadian symbol.
   _____
   _____

2. The black bear is a potentially dangerous animal often found in the wooded areas of Northern Canada.
   _____
   _____

3. Skiing is a popular winter sport in Canada.
   _____
   _____

4. Prince Edward Island has many popular tourist sites.
   _____
   _____

5. Aboriginal people are the original inhabitants of Canada.
   _____
   _____

6. Hockey is a popular sport in Canada.
   _____
   _____

Exercise E

Each paragraph is missing two sentences. Use the key words provided to create sentences that are examples of the general point.

1. Maple syrup is a delicious liquid made from the sap of sugar, red, and black maple trees found primarily in Ontario, Quebec, and New Brunswick. In the spring, people tap the trees by drilling a hole into the trunk and using a spout to collect the sap. The sap is then boiled for several hours to evaporate the water. The liquid that is left is a delicious sweet syrup that has many uses.
   (a) _____
   _____.
   It is not as thick as artificial pancake syrup, so you do not need to use as much, and it does not contain any chemicals or preservatives. Canada is the largest source of maple syrup, so visitors from around the world associate maple syrup as something uniquely Canadian.
   (b) _____
   _____.

   a) pour   pancakes and waffles   breakfast
   b) souvenir   popular   Canada

2. The dictionary defines a toboggan as a long, light, narrow sledge*, sometimes curved up in the front, used for sliding down hills. Traditionally, the First Nations people of Canada made toboggans of wooden slats that were curled up at the front in the shape of a sideways "J." The toboggan was a very useful means of transport. (a) _____

_____.

Modern toboggans are made from wood, aluminum, or plastic, but the shape is the same. Toboggans should not be confused with other traditional winter vehicles. (b) _____

_____.

A toboggan slides directly on the snow. Today, toboggans are mainly used for recreation. People love the thrill of sliding quickly through deep snow down a hill.

* vehicle that slides over snow

a) Aboriginal people   transport   people   supplies
b) toboggan   not sled / sleigh   skis on bottom

3. The thin layer of ice that forms on roads and sidewalks in winter is called black ice. It occurs when there is moisture or water on the surface that freezes. Black ice is very dangerous.
(a) _____

_____.

It looks like regular pavement or cement that is slightly shiny. It's not only easy for people walking to slip and fall on black ice, but many car accidents also result from black ice on roads.
(b) _____

_____.

Black ice is common in the winter in Canada.

a) Not thick layer   ice   easily see
b) drivers   too fast   cars   not stop

4. The term Mounties refers to the Royal Canadian Mounted Police. The RCMP is the national police force of Canada. It was formed in 1920 when two different police forces, the Northwest Mounted Police and the Dominion police, joined together. The Mountie uniform was inherited from the Northwest Mounted Police, which already had it in 1904, and it is still popular today.
(a) _____

_____.

The RCMP is unique in the world because it provides policing nationally, provincially, and municipally. The laws in a country show what the culture values and thinks is important. The job of the RCMP is to make sure that people follow Canada's laws and respect Canadian values. (b) _____

_____.

RCMP officers are often shown in movies and television as polite, determined, physically fit, and honest individuals who always "get their man." The men and women of the RCMP serve and protect the public.

a) people recognize   red jacket   brown hat
   leather boots   uniform   around the world
b) symbol   peace and order   Canadian culture

Exercise F

Write a definition paragraph for one of the topics in Exercises B or D. Use the Definition Paragraph Checklist as a guide.

✓ Definition Paragraph Checklist

Content

☐ Does my topic sentence state the item or idea that the paragraph will define?

☐ Does my topic sentence clearly identify whether my purpose is 1) to extend a formal dictionary definition, or 2) to give my interpretation of what the item or idea means?

☐ Have I included enough important features (qualities) of the item or idea to make its meaning clear?

☐ Have I used one or more of the following techniques to explain the item's important features: details or examples, comparisons, negation, origins, or uses?

Organization
- [ ] Do I begin with a short definition?
- [ ] Is my formal definition followed by the item's important features?

Meaning
- [ ] Have I used precise words to describe the thing being defined?
- [ ] Have I used words and phrases effectively to show the relationship between sentences?

Mechanics
- [ ] Have I checked my paragraph for mistakes in grammar, spelling, and punctuation?

Academic Word List

chapter	economic	location	statistics
cultures	goal	process	
define	issues	sum	

Word Meaning
Exercise A
Choose the correct meaning of the underlined word in each sentence.

1. The building of a national railroad that connected the eastern and western parts of the country was an important <u>chapter</u> in the story of Canada.
   a) sections of a book
   b) an important event or time in the history of something
   c) complete story

2. First Nations <u>cultures</u> are uniquely different from the European way of life that defined Canada in the past.
   a) groups with their own beliefs, art, language and ways of life
   b) the first people to live in a country
   c) the countries of Europe

3. The Canadian constitution is a document that describes the most important laws of Canada. According to the constitution, peace, order, and good government <u>define</u> us as Canadians.
   a) accurately describe what something or someone is
   b) paint a picture of something
   c) say the meaning of a word

4. The <u>economic</u> policies of a government are important because the wealth of a nation influences the quality of people's lives.
   a) connected with corruption in business
   b) connected with the trade, industry, and development of wealth
   c) connected with quality of life

5. In the early 1990s, the Canadian government set a <u>goal</u> of recruiting one percent of Canada's population from immigration.
   a) the net into which soccer players kick the ball
   b) a plan that one hopes to achieve
   c) a successful future

6. Job creation, health care, and education are three <u>issues</u> Canadians think about and debate at election time.
   a) editions of a magazine
   b) strategies for improving something
   c) important topics that people are discussing

7. The Plains of Abraham is the <u>location</u> where British soldiers defeated the French in 1759, leaving Quebec City under British control.
   a) a place outside a movie studio where scenes of a movie are filmed
   b) a place where something happens
   c) a place in the countryside that later becomes a city

8. Because of multiculturalism, Canadian culture is in the <u>process</u> of changing.
   a) a development that is not finished yet
   b) a change for the better
   c) a necessity to do something different

9. Canada is more than the <u>sum</u> of its 13 individual provinces and territories. It is a single, united country of more than 9,300,000 square kilometres with a landscape that ranges from mountains, prairies, and forests, to coastal and arctic landscapes.
   a) an amount of money
   b) the size of something
   c) the total number you get when you add two or more numbers together

10. The Canadian government collects information about its people (who they are, where they live, what jobs they have, and so on) and reports these <u>statistics</u> every four years.
    a) a collection of information shown in numbers
    b) information about jobs
    c) questions that research companies ask to collect information

Pronunciation
Exercise B
Listen to your teacher or an audio dictionary to hear the pronunciation of each word in the list. Repeat each word aloud. Mark the syllables and major word stress.

1. chapter (n)   **cháp** / ter
2. culture (n)   _____
3. define (v)   _____
4. economic (adj)   _____
5. goal (n)   _____
6. issue (n)   _____
7. location (n)   _____
8. process (n)   _____
9. sum (n)   _____
10. statistics (n)   _____

Word Forms
Exercise C
Fill in each blank with the word form shown in parentheses. Select only word forms that have the same meaning as in Exercise A.

1. chapter (n)
2. culture (n): _____ (adj)
    _____ (adv)
3. define (v): _____ (n)
4. economic (adj): _____ (n)
    _____ (adv)
    _____ (adj)
5. goal (n)
6. issue (n)
7. location (n): _____ (v)
8. process (n): _____ (v)
    _____ (adj)
9. sum (n): _____ (v)
    _____ (v)
    _____ (n)
10. statistics (n): _____ (adj)
    _____ (adv)

Exercise D
In a dictionary, find one example sentence for each word in Exercise A and copy it into your notebook. Write a second sentence of your own. Then, work with a partner to revise and edit your sentences.

Exercise E
Read about Black Loyalists in Canada and fill in the blanks with words from the list.

| chapter | define | located |
| cultural | goal | statistics |

It is difficult to ₁_____ what it means to be Canadian. Many ₂_____ groups from around the world have helped to build the nation of Canada. One important ₃_____ in the story of Canadian history is the arrival and contribution of Black Loyalists who ₄_____ in Nova Scotia. During the years from 1775 to 1783, the young nation that later became the United States fought for its independence from Britain. This event was known as the American Revolution. Thousands of people who were loyal to Britain were forced to flee and many of them were black. To achieve their ₅_____ of victory in the war, the British had promised Black Loyalists freedom if they fought on the British side. Thirty thousand blacks escaped from slavery to fight for the British. They worked as soldiers, labourers, ships' pilots, and cooks. The British kept accurate ₆_____ on births, deaths, and marriages. That's how we know that more than 2000 Black Loyalists were sent to Canada when it became clear that the British were going to lose the war.

| economic | issues | process | sum |

They arrived in the town of Shelburne in southeastern Nova Scotia. About 2500 blacks formed the settlement of Birchtown, the largest settlement of free blacks outside Africa. Most Black Loyalists never received the land or provisions they had been promised. They were forced to earn low wages as farm hands or domestic workers. Poor living conditions, disease, and the ₇_____ devastation of poverty were serious ₈_____ at Birchtown. In 1791, a British company offered to relocate the black settlers to Sierra Leone in West Africa. Almost half the black community of Nova Scotia left. A ₉_____ of approximately 2500 remained. Through the gradual ₁₀_____ of qualifying for skilled trades, wages rose, and their situation slowly improved.

Answer Key

Unit 1

Vocabulary

Exercise A

1. selfless
2. persistent
3. honest
4. well-respected
5. dedicated
6. trustworthy
7. innovative

Exercise B

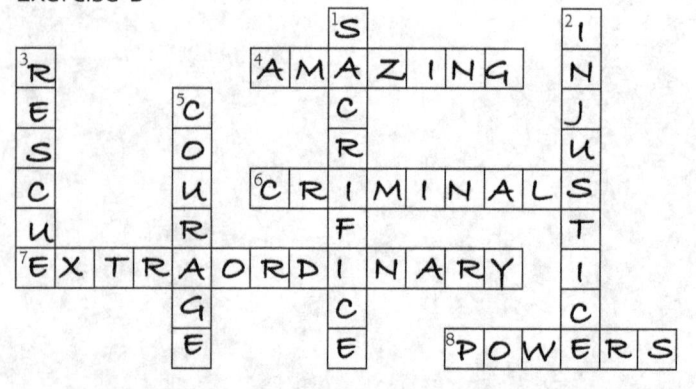

Crossword:
- 3 Down: RESCUE
- 4 Across: AMAZING
- 5 Down: COURAGE
- 1 Down: SACRIFICE
- 2 Down: INJUSTIC(E)
- 6 Across: CRIMINALS
- 7 Across: EXTRAORDINARY
- 8 Across: POWERS

Vocabulary Expansion

Exercise C

1. violent
2. cruel
3. reviled
4. self-centred
5. uncommitted
6. corrupt
7. dishonest
8. cowardice

Exercise D

1. corrupt
2. cruel
3. self-centred
4. dishonest
5. cowardice
6. violent
7. uncommitted
8. reviled

Grammar Focus

Exercise A

1. consistently
2. tirelessly
3. incredibly
4. determinedly
5. continuously
6. steadfastly
7. skilfully
8. unwaveringly
9. purposefully
10. speedily

Exercise B

1. b
2. a
3. e
4. a
5. b
6. b
7. a
8. d
9. c
10. a

Exercise C

1. He drives carefully.
2. She teaches excellently.
3. She dances gracefully.
4. He studies eagerly.
5. She reads silently.
6. He fights fires proudly.
7. She skates naturally.
8. He plays defensively.

Grammar Edit

When I think of heroes, I think of individuals who have sacrificed everything so that the people in their country can be free. One of my heroes is Aung San Suu Kyi. Her father was a national hero who brave (**bravely**) fought to free Burma from British domination. She followed in his footsteps determined (**determinedly**) fighting the military regime that took over after the British left. She was democratic (**democratically**) elected and should be the prime minister of Myanmar (formerly called Burma), but the powerful military unlawful (**unlawfully**) refused to recognize the vote. They thought that she was a threat to their power and placed her under house arrest. She was famous (**famously**) awarded the Nobel Peace Prize for her non-violent struggles for freedom. She is a freedom fighter who has never given up her beliefs or resorted to violence in her fight for democracy—that's why she is my hero.

Reading

Guided Summary

Answers will vary, but should have the same meaning as the model below.

A woman and her baby <u>are trapped in a burning building</u>. They <u>are rescued</u> by Superman. Superheroes <u>are amazing</u> because of <u>their great qualities</u>. They make personal <u>sacrifices</u> to save others from <u>danger</u>. Their amazing skills come from different sources. Some superheroes <u>were born</u> with their powers. Some got their powers as a result of <u>an accident</u>. Some are actually <u>aliens from other planets</u>. Other superheroes create and use <u>high-tech gadgets</u> to fight the bad guys. Superheroes have <u>characteristics</u> with which we identify. Often they live like <u>ordinary people</u> in our society. We can easily relate to this second identity. Kids today see superheroes when they go <u>to the movies</u>. Computer special effects let everyone's imagination come to life. We can see our favourite <u>movie stars</u> fighting evil. The movies remind us of simpler times when good would win <u>over evil</u>.

Writing

Model Paragraph

1. The writer is trying to tell a story of a time he felt like a hero.
2. The story is about the author and his neighbours. It took place at 2:00 a.m. on a cold Saturday morning. The writer was walking home and saw flames coming from a neighbour's house. He got them out of the house.
3. The information is in chronological order.
4. The transitional expressions are: *when*, *as*, and *later*.
5. There is no information in the story that does not support the main idea.

Exercise A

a2, b7, c4, d1, e6, f8, g3, h5

Topic Sentence: When I was a child, I wanted to be just like Superman, my favourite superhero.

Exercise C

Possible answers:
1. When
2. Later, After a while
3. after
4. First, At first
5. Then, Soon, Later
6. Now, Today

Academic Word List

Exercise A

1. motivate
2. series
3. physical
4. generate
5. source
6. alter
7. job
8. element
9. recover
10. attribute

Exercise B

2. **àt** / tri / bute
3. **èl** / e / ment
4. **gèn** / er / ate
5. **jòb**
6. **mò** / ti / vate
7. **phỳs** / i / cal
8. re / **còv** / er
9. **sèr** / ies
10. **sòurce**

Exercise C

1. alter (v): altered (adj) alteration (n) alternative (adj)
2. attribute (n): attribution (n) attribute (v)
3. element (n): elemental (adj)
4. generate (v): generator (n) generated (adj)
5. job (n): jobless (adj—neg)
6. motivate (v): motivation (n) motive (n) motivated (adj) motivating (adj) motivational (adj)
7. physical (adj): physically (adv) physique (n)
8. recover (v): recovering (adj) recovery (n)
9. series (n): serial (adj)
10. source (n): source (v)

Exercise E

1. series
2. job
3. alter
4. elements
5. source
6. physical
7. attributes
8. recover
9. motivated
10. generated

Unit 2

Vocabulary

Exercise A

1. code
2. reveal
3. mystery
4. excavation
5. proof
6. forgeries
7. ancient
8. secret
9. hoax
10. archaeology
11. society
12. rituals
13. speculation
14. theory
15. conspiracy

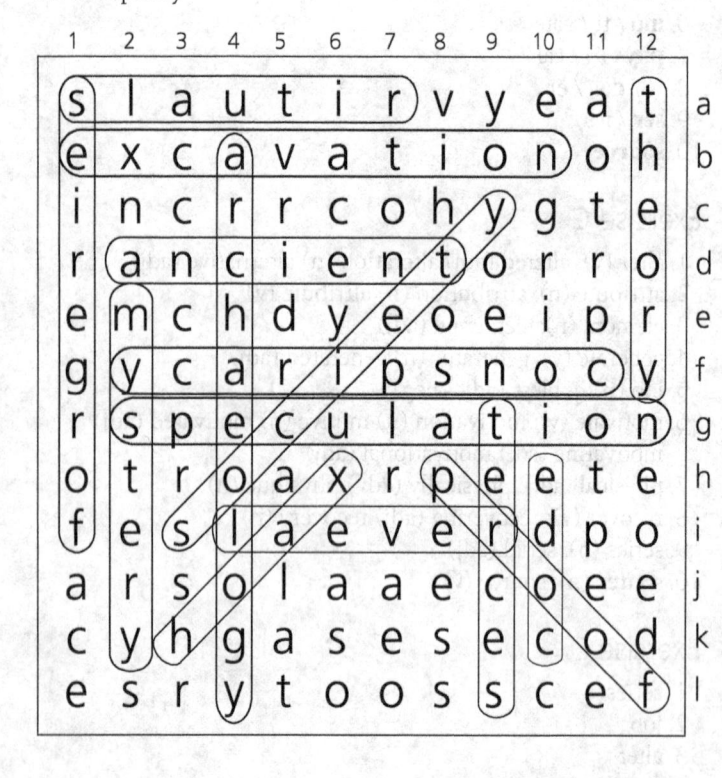

Exercise B

The study of peoples and their cultures, which can include the ^ of long-forgotten cities, is called ^. People who are interested in finding out about an ^ civilization can read about the discoveries in the blogs of archaeologists. They used to keep their discoveries a ^ because they didn't want others to come to the site before they had uncovered enough ^ to clearly support their ^ of who lived there in ancient times. Of course not all finds are real. Some are in fact skillful ^ that some dishonest person has "discovered"	(n) excavation (n) archaeology (adj) ancient (n) secret (n) proof (n) theory (n) forgeries
in hopes of becoming famous or rich. Careful scientific examinations sometimes ^ that someone has tried to pull an elaborate ^ on the public. Because of this planned fraud, there is always ^ about the validity of any new claim when something amazing is discovered. There is still a lot of ^ associated with the ancient pyramids of Egypt. We can speculate about some of the ^ performed in the pyramids. Do the members of the secret ^ of the Freemasons know the pyramid's secrets? They are all sworn to a ^ of silence and are not allowed to tell anyone what they actually know. Some people believe that there is a ^ by the Freemasons to rule the world with the secret knowledge and wealth they have acquired.	(v) reveal (n) hoax (n) speculation (n) mystery (n) rituals (n) society (n) code (n) conspiracy

Grammar Focus

Exercise A

1. created
2. made
3. constructed
4. used
5. weren't able
6. was flying, rediscovered
7. proposed
8. were landing, used
9. piled
10. believed, lived, looked

Exercise B

Kira: Did you visit San Agustin when you went to Colombia last summer?
Manjit: Yes, it was amazing.

Kira: Did you see the giant stone statues?
Manjit: Yes, they had terrifying faces. Many looked part human and part jaguar.

Kira: I heard that they are the largest group of megalithic statues in South America.
Manjit: Yes. That's what the tour guide told us.

Kira: Many are next to burial sites, aren't they?
Manjit: Yes. In 1913, German archaeologist Konrad Theodor Preuss discovered tombs that contained people buried with lots of gold and silver.

Kira: Were the statues built to protect the tombs?
Manjit: That's what many people believe.

Kira: Who built the statues?
Manjit: Experts believe that people from an ancient civilization built them and then disappeared before the Europeans arrived in the 1500s.

Exercise C

1. The Knights Templar kept people's money safe while they were travelling to the Holy Land.
2. A farmer claimed that he found the Ica stones while he was exploring some local caves.
3. Strange patterns appeared in the farmer's field while he was sleeping.
4. A team discovered pieces of a marble statue while digging in an ancient city.
5. A man found mastodon bones while digging a ditch on his uncle's farm.
6. A woman found some fossilized bones while cleaning the attic.
7. Ash buried thousands of people alive while they were fleeing from the volcano.
8. Archaeologists discovered human remains while they were excavating the ruins.
9. Ninjas slowed their breathing while they were waiting for their victim to sleep.
10. Ninjas dripped poison down a string into their victim's mouth while the victim was sleeping.

Grammar Edit

The police were arresting (**arrested**) a farmer in a small village outside of Rome when they discovered treasures hidden in his house. The archaeological police become (**became**) suspicious a few weeks earlier when they were seeing (**saw**) fresh piles of dirt next to the river. While they investigated (**were investigating**), they found small pieces of broken pottery. The police were watched (**watched**) the farmer digging for several days. When they were going (**went**) to his house, they found more than 500 fragile miniature pots made approximately 2600 years ago. The jars were made between the seventh and fifth centuries BCE. The farmer breaking (**broke**) Italian laws by not reporting that he had found the ancient artifacts immediately to the authorities. That is why they arrested him.

Archaeologists believe that people living in the area throw (**threw**) the pottery into the river during festivities as offerings to deities. These pots were symbols of storage and cooking pots were using (**used**) in daily life. Italy has very strict laws about individuals finding and keeping ancient artifacts. They make (**made**) it a law years ago because at the time they wanted archaeologists to investigate these finds to learn more about the people from these ancient cultures.

Reading

Guided Summary

Answers will vary, but should have the same meaning as the model below.

Japanese ninjas were paid assassins who lived in the sixteenth century. They used disguises to keep from being discovered so they could move around easily. They trained their breathing so they could stay still for days and they trained their eyes to see in the dark. They used poison to kill silently. They passed their secrets only to their sons.

Freemasons were skilled craftsman who built large cathedrals, temples, and castles in the late sixteenth century. They also knew about the secrets of the buildings they constructed. There were many levels in the society and each level had secret knowledge. Churches didn't like that this organization was not religious. The Freemasons used rituals and secret greetings to protect their knowledge from others.

Writing

Model Paragraph

1. The writer is comparing the pyramids in Egypt and Mexico.
2. The topic is pyramids. The topic sentence is: The Great Pyramid of Giza in Egypt and the Great Pyramid of Cholula in Mexico are both world famous monuments, but there are several significant differences between them.
3. The comparison points are organized in a point-by-point format.
4. The following words are used to show similarities and differences: *one major difference is, on the other hand, also differ, in contrast, the final major difference, this differs from, both.*
5. The signal words are: *also differ, the final major difference is.*

Exercise A

Comparison Word(s)	Contrast Word(s)
both, likewise, also, just as	but, whereas, unlike, is different from, while, differs from

Exercise B

	Pompeii	Angkor
1.	a partially excavated Roman city near Naples, Italy. Includes ruins of an amphitheatre, swimming pool, aqueduct, public baths, private houses, and businesses	thousands of temples mostly in ruins located in Cambodia. Includes Angkor Wat, one of the most famous ruins in the world
2.	destroyed and completely buried by a volcanic eruption in 79 CE	abandoned in the fifteenth century when invaded by Thai invaders
3.	excavation began in 1748 and has continued in several different phases to the present.	restoration process began in 1907 and continues to present day, with a brief work stoppage during the civil war in the 1970s
4.	visited by more than 2 million people every year	visited by up to a million people a year.
5.	city built mainly during the Augustan period (27 BCE to 14 CE)	Hindu empire built in the early twelfth century
6.	covered by a thick layer of ash and soil, rediscovered in 1599, and then again in 1738	covered over by the thick jungle and rediscovered in 1860 by French explorer Henri Mouhot
7.	Pompeii is the biggest tourist attraction in Italy.	Angkor Wat is the largest religious monument in the world.

Exercise C
Point-by-point Comparison

Point 1	*location*
Pompeii	Italy
Angkor	Cambodia
Point 2	***purposes for the types of buildings***
Pompeii	amphitheatre, aqueduct, houses, businesses
Angkor	all temples
Point 3	***reasons locations abandoned***
Pompeii	volcanic eruption
Angkor	invasion by the Thai

Block-method Comparison

Details about Pompeii
Excavation history
excavation began in 1748 and has continued in several different phases to the present
Popularity
visited by more than 2 million people every year.
Rediscovery
covered by a thick layer of ash and soil, rediscovered in 1599, and then again in 1738

Details about Angkor
Excavation history
restoration process began in 1907 and continues to present day, with a brief work stoppage during the civil war in the 1970s
Popularity
visited by up to 1 million people every year
Rediscovery
covered over by the thick jungle and rediscovered in 1860 by French explorer Henri Mouhot

Exercise D
Possible answer:
Topic Sentence: Pompeii and Angkor are different in many ways.

Exercise E
1. Unlike Pompeii, Angkor is located in Asia.
2. One way Pompeii is different from Angkor is the purpose of the buildings.
3. Angkor is different from Pompeii because of what happened to the inhabitants.
4. Pompeii is similar to Angkor in that they are both still being excavated.
5. Like Angkor, Pompeii is a popular tourist destination.
6. One way Pompeii is similar to Angkor is that they were both rediscovered after being forgotten for a long period of time.

Academic Word List

Exercise A
1. a
2. c
3. b
4. a
5. b
6. c
7. c
8. b
9. a
10. c

Exercise B
2. con / **strŭc** / tion
3. de / **sign** / ers
4. **ĕth** / nic
5. **ĕv** / i / dence
6. **ĕx** / pert
7. i / **dĕn** / ti / fy
8. pro / **fĕs** / sion / al
9. **prŏ** / jects
10. re / **quire**

Exercise C
1. consequently (adv): consequent (adj) consequential (adj) consequence (n)
2. construction (n): construct (v)
3. designers (n): design (v) designed (adj) design (n)
4. ethnic (adj): ethnically (adv) ethnicity (n)
5. evidence (n): evident (adj) evidently (adv)
6. expert (n): expertly (adv) expertise (n)
7. identify (v): identifiable (adj) identification (n)
8. professional (adj): professionalism (n) professional (n) professionally (adv)
9. projects (n): project (v)
10. require (v): requirement (n) required (adj)

Exercise E
1. construction
2. expert
3. identify
4. evidence
5. ethnic
6. consequently
7. designers
8. require
9. professional
10. projects

Unit 3

Vocabulary

Exercise A
1. provinces
2. Maritimes
3. Prairie
4. coasts
5. territories
6. mountains
7. natural resources
8. forests
9. valleys
10. tundra
11. arctic
12. flatlands
13. borders
14. regions
15. landscapes

Exercise B
1. provinces
2. territories
3. coast
4. Maritime
5. forest
6. regions
7. natural resources
8. Prairie
9. flatlands
10. landscapes
11. mountains
12. valley
13. borders
14. Arctic
15. tundra

Grammar Focus

Exercise A
1. many
2. most
3. every
4. more
5. each
6. either
7. some
8. several
9. both
10. few

Exercise B
1. much
2. little
3. a few
4. many
5. few
6. many
7. a little
8. little

Exercise C
2. Both are capital cities.
3. Most live close to the US border.
4. More people live in Ontario.
5. All the provinces have a provincial flag. / Each province has a provincial flag. / Every province has a provincial flag.
6. Few people live in the Arctic.
7. All adult Canadians know the words to "O Canada." or Every/Each adult Canadian knows the words to "O Canada."
8. Neither province has tundra.

Grammar Edit

The Canadian Rockies are part of the North American Rocky Mountain range. The Rockies cover parts of each (**both**) Alberta and British Columbia. Much of the Canadian Rockies are (**is**) composed of layered sedimentary rock such as limestone and shale. There is (**are**) several national parks in the Rockies including Jasper, Banff, Kootenay, Yoho, and Waterton. Four of these national parks and three provincial parks are UNESCO World Heritage sites. Many (**Much**) of the mountain range is protected by the parks. The mountains are a popular tourist destination. A few (**Few**) people fail to be impressed by the natural beauty of the Rockies—it's impossible not to be wowed. If you like to hike and camp, there is (**are**) some alpine huts throughout the Rockies where you can sleep or have a rest. There are most (**many**) rivers and lakes where you can fish. Every year, a little (**few**) adventurers attempt to climb Mount Robson and Mount Columbia. Outdoor enthusiasts go there to neither (**either**) ski or snowboard on the majestic slopes. Many people takes (**take**) the two-day scenic train ride through the Canadian Rockies every year.

Guided Summary

	People	Geology	Climate	Industry
The North	mostly Aboriginal	lowlands, mountain ranges, tundra	short summer, long, cold, dark winter	mining, oil and gas, tourism
Pacific Coast	people of Chinese and European descent, Asians people from other parts of world	coast mountains	wet and mild dry	tourism, mining, fishing, agriculture, forestry

The Prairies	prairie farmers	Rocky Mountains flatlands rivers, lakes, forests, bogs Canadian Shield	Chinook winds	agriculture forestry mining manufacturing
Central Canada	new immigrants the French (Quebecois)	lowlands Canadian Shield	warmer, less extreme warm summers, long cold winters sub arctic arctic	financial industries manufacturing hydroelectric generation agriculture mining forestry
The Atlantic Coast	settlers from France, the British Isles, Germany, & Black settlers from the United States	rolling hills natural beauty forested rugged ocean coast subarctic	changing weather lots of precipitation	agriculture tourism fishing forestry mining ship building

Writing

Model Paragraph

1. The writer is trying to describe a beautiful scene.
2. The topic is a beautiful nature scene. The topic sentence is: The view from the rocky cliff where we have stopped for a rest while hiking is absolutely breathtaking.
3. The writer's point of view is that it is spectacular. "Absolutely breathtaking" indicates this.
4. Touch: rocky, cool; Sight: tall, large, tiny; Smell: fragrant
5. d) centre to outside. The writer first describes the centre of the lake and then describes what surrounds it moving from the shore, then up the hills.

Exercise B

Possible answers:

1. unmistakeable (impression) aroma (smell) favourite (impression) wafted (smell)
2. Sweet (taste) golden maple syrup drips (sight) generously (impression) steaming pancakes (sight)
3. crystal vase (sight) five bright pink tulips (sight) decorates (sight)
4. morning news (hearing) speakers (hearing) strategically (impression) placed (sight)
5. excited chirping (hearing) of birds (sight) perched (sight) shady tree (sight) drifts (hearing)
6. smell (smell) freshly brewed coffee (smell) competes (impression) sweet (taste) smell of the pancakes (smell)
7. grasp (touch) smooth (touch) comfortable (impression) ceramic handle (touch) favourite (impression) raise (touch)
8. love (emotion) taste (taste) of strong (taste) dark-roast (sight)

Exercise D

On one end of my coffee table sits a carving—an amazing gift I received last year from an artist friend originally from Yellowknife. The carving is of an Inuit hunter hunting a bear. It is made from Brazilian soapstone, which has rich and varied shades of brown. The base of the statue is a rough, unfinished slab of soapstone. On the right, the hunter is ready to attack. In front of him, a large polar bear is trying to escape. The hunter is wearing a thick warm parka. His face is partially hidden by the thick furry hood that surrounds his face. Below his parka you can see that he is wearing warm leggings made from animal skins. His feet, which are firmly planted on the rock, are covered in warm moccasin-like boots. Clutched in his right hand is a roughly cut stick with a long thin sharpened stone tied to it like a hammer. The bear is leaning to the left as if it is trying to escape the hunter. Its enormous paws look as if they could kill the hunter with one single swipe. I think that the carving represents survival. It is a real conversation starter for anyone visiting my house.

Exercise E

d, a, e, h, g, f, c, b
Note: Other answers may be possible as long as they make sense

Academic Word List

Exercise A

1. h
2. j / d
3. c
4. a
5. g
6. b
7. f
8. i
9. e
10. d / j

Exercise B

2. **brief**
3. de / **bàte**
4. ex / **pòse**
5. fi / **nàn** / cial
6. **rànge**
7. **im** / mi / grant
8. **mà** / jor
9. par / **tic** / i / pate
10. re / **vèal**

Exercise C

1. area (n): no other common forms with this meaning
2. brief (adj): briefly (adv)
3. debate (n) debate (v) debatable (adj)
4. expose (v): exposure (n) exposed (adj)
5. financial (adj): finance (n) finance (v)
6. range (n): range (v)
7. immigrant (n): immigrant (adj) immigrate (v) immigration (n)
8. major (adj): major (n) major (v)
9. participate (v): participant (n) participation (n) participatory (adj)
10. reveal (v): revelation (n) revealing (adj)

Exercise E

1. major
2. immigrants
3. area
4. ranges
5. financial
6. brief
7. participate
8. expose
9. debate
10. revealed

Unit 4

Vocabulary

Exercise A
1. networking
2. trend
3. features
4. devices
5. blog
6. communities
7. connect
8. hype
9. gaming
10. genre
11. lurking
12. media
13. tweets
14. texting
15. celebrities

Exercise B
1. celebrities
2. media
3. hype
4. devices
5. blogs
6. networking
7. community
8. connect
9. tweet
10. features

Vocabulary Expansion

Exercise C
Possible answers:
1. digital media, electronic media, ethnic media, global media, local media, mass media, online media, social media; *media gossip, media habits, media hype*
2. computer device(s), digital device(s), electronic device(s), mechanical device(s) safety device(s), wireless device(s)
3. computer network(s), digital network(s), electronic network(s), global network(s), local network(s), online network(s), social network(s), wireless network(s)
4. *community support*, global community, local community, online community, social community
5. *celebrity gossip, celebrity worship*, global celebrity(ies), local celebrity(ies), online celebrity(ies)
6. electronic connection, online connection, social connection, wireless connection
7. fashion trend(s), global trend(s), local trend(s), online trend(s), social trend(s)

Exercise D
1. global
2. social
3. electronic / digital / computer
4. community / local
5. media
6. social / support
7. digital / online / social
8. wireless
9. media
10. celebrity

Grammar Focus

Exercise A
Possible answers:
1. I don't know how people can live without the Internet.
2. My mother is worried about how much time I spend online.
3. I'm not worried about Internet safety.
4. The average age of computer- and video-game players is 35.
5. I rely on the Internet to get the latest news.
6. I put a time limit on my kids' video-game playing.
7. I'm going to buy a new cellphone soon.
8. I think I'm addicted to texting.

Exercise B
1. I don't follow the latest trends. (lines 5–6)
2. I can't imagine spending more than $1.50 for a cup of coffee. (lines 6–7)
3. I don't need twenty choices of coffee with latte, soy, or whipped cream. (lines 7–9)
4. I miss the small community where my parents and my sister still live. (lines 11–13)
5. Before I became famous I worked / had worked as a waiter. (lines 17–18)
6. I had to work hard for little pay. (lines 18–19)

Exercise C
1. He asked if I read the newspaper.
2. He asked if she read entertainment blogs.
3. They asked if I had a cellphone contract.
4. The researcher asked how many text messages they sent and received every day.
5. His mother asked when he stopped playing video games.
6. His friend asked where he bought that digital device.
7. She asked who read celebrity gossip blogs.
8. She asked how many friends were on my social-networking site.
9. The teacher asked what online communities we belonged to.
10. The professor asked why social connections were so important.

Exercise D
1. The interviewer asked the group how many hours per week they spent playing computer games.

2. The interviewer asked one young woman if she had more face-to-face friends or more online friends.
3. The interviewer asked the group if they tweeted.
4. The interviewer asked one young man what genres of television programs he liked best.
5. The interviewer asked one man what his favourite online game was.
6. The interviewer asked one woman when she went to sleep at night.
7. The interviewer asked one woman where she got information about her favourite celebrity.
8. The interviewer asked the group if they listened to the radio.
9. The interviewer asked one young woman why she preferred texting to calling.
10. The interviewer asked the group who their favourite bloggers were.

Exercise E

Answers may vary. Tenses may vary according to intended meaning.
Possible answers:
1. The man said he spent about 20 hours per week playing computer games.
2. The young woman reported that she had a lot more online friends than face-to face friends.
3. The young woman said she just started tweeting last week.
4. The young man said he liked drama shows.
5. The young man said he didn't have one favourite online game. He liked several.
6. The young man said that on a weeknight he went to sleep around midnight.
7. The woman said that she got information about her favourite celebrities from their websites.
8. The man reported that he listened to the radio sometimes.
9. The young woman said she preferred texting to calling because it was cheaper.
10. The woman said that she loved Corey Doctorow's tech blog.

Grammar Edit

₁ The blogger asked that (**if**) he was addicted to the Internet and his phone. ₂ He reported that he decided to write down how often he used his phone and the Internet. ₃ He said during the week he read the news online while I (**he**) ate breakfast. ₄ He said that he checked for personal voicemail or text messages on his cellphone on the way to work on the bus. ₅ He said that when he got to the office, he checked his phone messages. ₆ Then he spent about half an hour reading and answering my (**his**) work email. ₇ He reported that last week, I (**he**) spent three hours of my (**his**) day looking up information for work. ₈ He asked (**said**) if no one is in the lunchroom when he eats his lunch, he checks what his Facebook friends are doing. ₉ He reported that last week no one was in the lunchroom all week. ₁₀ He said if (**that or Ø**) the bus ride home is boring so he always plays a few games on his phone. ₁₁ The blogger said my (**his**) wife called him on the way home on Friday. ₁₂ She asked if do you want (**he wanted**) to go out for dinner? ₁₃ He asked where did she want (**she wanted**) to go. ₁₄ He said that they met at a little Italian restaurant. ₁₅ He admitted that during dinner he received three text messages and she made two phone calls.

Guided Summary

Wording may vary, but content should include the following.

People often think that teens do not use ₁ traditional media like radio and television anymore because they prefer new media. This is not true. Research tells us that teens use new media ₂ in addition to traditional media. ₃ Television is still the most common medium for teens. ₄ Reality or ₅ participation/variety programs are very popular with teenagers around the world. It is also not true that teens spend more time on computers than ₆ other age groups. On the contrary, they spend ₇ less time on computers and the Internet than other age groups. In the United States, teens spend about ₈ half as much time on the Web per month than the overall US ₉ average. It is also a myth that teens only ₁₀ text with their cellphones now. Teens do text a lot, but they also use many different ₁₁ mobile data features. They download ringtones, games, and applications. They instant message and use the mobile Web. Finally, teens are also not the biggest ₁₂ gamers of all age groups. Over the last two decades, the gaming audience has grown to include new groups of users, including ₁₃ girls, children, and older people. Overall, the research shows that the media habits of teens are ₁₄ not very different from the media habits of ₁₅ the total population.

Writing

Model Paragraph

1. The writer is trying to persuade the reader; The writer wants the reader to agree with his or her opinion.
2. Topic: the amount of time teens spend using electronic media
   Topic sentence: The amount of time teens spend using electronic media is endangering their physical and emotional health.
3. The writer's view is that using electronic media "is endangering their physical and emotional health."
4. The writer uses the following types of evidence:
   - Facts: e.g., The study does not directly connect time spent in front of a television or computer screen with poorer health.
   - Statistics: e.g., A recent study by the Centre for Addiction and Mental Health shows that hundreds of thousands of teens spend at least seven hours a day staring at a computer or TV screen.
   - Expert opinion: e.g., experts such as Dr. Mann
   - Common sense: e.g., When teens are sitting in front of a screen, they're not physically active.

Exercise A

1. Topic: social networking's influence on friendships
   Controlling idea: dramatically changing them
2. Topic: traditional media in digital world
   Controlling idea: will not survive
3. Topic: smart phones' influence on computers
   Controlling idea: making computers unnecessary

4. Topic: Internet's influence on reading
   Controlling idea: improves
5. Topic: our obsession with daily lives of celebrities
   Controlling idea: caused by the Internet
6. Topic: computers' influence on us
   Controlling idea: making us lazy
7. Topic: young people's ability to have healthy sexual relationships
   Controlling idea: destroyed by Internet porn
8. Topic: how we communicate
   Controlling idea: changing because of online communication
9. Topic: online youth and privacy
   Controlling idea: not valued
10. Topic: Internet generation
    Controlling idea: more sophisticated

Exercise B
1. ✔
2. ✔
3. ✘ (c: too general)
4. ✔
5. ✔
6. ✘ (a: fact/ no point of view)
7. ✘ (a: fact/no point of view)
8. ✘ (b: grammatically incomplete)
9. ✔
10. ✘ (c: too general)
11. ✘ (a and d: fact / too specific)
12. ✔

Exercise D
Outline 1
~~Youth should get part-time jobs to earn some money.~~
~~If they don't do well in school, they will not get a job.~~
~~They should do more sports, play music and read books.~~

Outline 2
~~Emotions of contestants are more natural than emotions of professional actors.~~
~~Writers must write many drafts before they have a script; takes time; professional writers are expensive.~~
~~More interesting to film in a real-life location.~~

Academic Word List

Exercise A
1. g
2. e
3. j
4. f
5. i
6. b
7. c
8. h
9. a
10. d

Exercise B
2. com / **mù** / ni / cate
3. **dà** / ta
4. o / ver / **àll**
5. per / **cènt**
6. **ròle**
7. **sùr** / vey
8. **tàsk**
9. tech / **nò** / lo / gy
10. tra / **di** / tio / nal

Exercise C
1. access (n) access (v) accessible (adj) accessibility (n)
2. communicate (v) communicative (adj) communication (n) communicator (n)
3. data (n pl) no other common form with this meaning
4. overall (adv) overall (adj)
5. percent (n) percentage (n)
6. role (n) no other common form with this meaning
7. survey (n) survey (v)
8. task (n) no other common form with this meaning
9. technology (n) technological (adj) technologically (adv) technologist (n)
10. traditional (adj) traditionally (adv) tradition (n)

Exercise E
1. traditionally
2. access
3. technology
4. overall
5. role
6. communication
7. percentage
8. data
9. surveyed
10. task

Unit 5

Vocabulary

Exercise A

1. sales pitch
2. retail
3. contract
4. receipt
5. deal / discount
6. knock-offs
7. discount / deal
8. store credit
9. refund
10. warranty

Exercise B

1. scam
2. telemarketer
3. recall
4. receipt
5. counterfeit
6. discount, deal, or promotion
7. refund
8. consumer
9. contract
10. store credit

Vocabulary Expansion

Exercise C

1. barefaced liar: someone who lies easily, with a total lack of shame
2. bend the truth: say something that is not entirely true
3. black market: illegal buying and selling of goods
4. catch someone red-handed: caught while doing something wrong or illegal
5. five-finger discount: stealing
6. lie through your teeth: lie openly knowing that what you are saying is completely false
7. pack of lies: a large number of untruthful statements
8. pull a fast one: gain an advantage over someone by deceiving them
9. rip you off: charge you more than they should
10. take to the cleaners: make someone lose a lot of money in an unfair way.

Exercise D

lie: barefaced liar, bend the truth, lie through your teeth, pack of lies

cheat: black market, pull a fast one, take to the cleaners, catch someone red-handed, rip you off

steal: catch someone red-handed, five-finger discount, rip you off

Exercise E

1. pack of lies
2. five-finger discount
3. taken to the cleaners / ripped off
4. bent the truth
5. black market
6. pulled a fast one / ripped me off
7. ripped me off / pulled a fast one
8. barefaced liar
9. lying through my teeth / bending the truth
10. caught the kid red-handed

Grammar Focus

Exercise A

1. driving
2. working
3. eating
4. learning
5. getting
6. finding
7. telling
8. shopping

Exercise B

Possible answers:
1. The most interesting sport is boxing.
2. His favourite activity is reading.
3. Convincing people to purchase knock-offs is easy.
4. My idea of a good time is eating at a nice restaurant.
5. Purchasing a TV was thrilling.
6. Finding a bargain is exciting.
7. Getting ripped off was aggravating.
8. Catching a thief is rewarding.

Exercise C

Possible answers:
1. arresting
2. identifying
3. falling
4. contacting
5. transferring
6. sending
7. asking
8. losing

Exercise D

Possible answers:
1. getting
2. cheating / scamming
3. checking
4. believing
5. paying
6. hearing
7. purchasing
8. getting

Exercise E

1. Janice is concerned about identifying counterfeit purses.
2. Mike is good at determining if someone is lying.
3. He is tired of shopping every day after work.
4. I'm afraid of getting ripped off.
5. She is worried about getting caught stealing.
6. The video tape should be suitable for identifying the thief.
7. Kim was excited about taking/planning a great trip.
8. Hakim is responsible for keeping track of the goods stolen each week.

Exercise F

1. about buying
2. at finding
3. on checking
4. about getting
5. about having
6. by having / at having
7. in doing
8. of stealing
9. for lying
10. to visiting

Grammar Edit

1. **Stuffing Envelopes at Home**
   For a small fee a company promises to show you how to earn money while working at home. Avoid ~~get~~ (**getting**) scammed. All you get for your money is a letter telling you to place similar ads (at your expense) to recruit others. If you do this, you are responsible for ~~scam~~ (**scamming**) other innocent people.

2. **Assembly or Craft Work at Home**
   The ads propose ~~make~~ (**making**) lots of money for goods you either make or put together at home. The person you contact strongly advises ~~buy~~ (**buying**) expensive materials and equipment from the company first that are necessary to get started. Then the company never ends up ~~purchase~~ (**purchasing**) the items you have made. You never get your investment money back or earn any extra. ~~Pay~~ (**Paying**) for the necessary materials is a scam.

3. **Computer Work at Home**
   A company claims you can earn money doing data entry and word processing from home. After you contact the company, it insists on ~~receive~~ (**receiving**) a small fee for the initial set-up. People report ~~get~~ (**getting**) a useless guide with only a few business contacts in companies that are not legitimate or pay very little.

4. **Pyramid Schemes**
   You get excited about ~~make~~ (**making**) big money selling products. You earn commissions on your own sales. The company also strongly recommends ~~recruit~~ (**recruiting**) others, so you can earn commissions from their sales as well. Only the people at the top (those that began this distribution chain) make any real money.

   Don't risk ~~lose~~ (**losing**) your money. ~~Get~~ (**Getting**) scammed is frustrating. Legitimate companies don't require fees to get further information or try to pressure you to make a fast decision. If you come across one of these ads offering to give you big money for little effort or the opportunity to get rich quick, ignore it. Chances are it is just another version of these popular successful scams.

Guided Summary

"Ways Stores Get You to Spend More Money Than You Think"

1. Retailers use many ways to get consumers to buy items, but consumers often misunderstand the true value of the sales approaches used.
2. **Double discount:** Calculating a second discount on the first discounted price. Consumers add the two together and take off the total instead of calculating the second discount on the first discounted price.

   Buy One, Get One Free: Receiving a free item when the same item is purchased at full price. The cost of the item may have been increased so the second item is not really free.

   Sale Price: The price an item is selling for appears to be discounted. The price may be the same as the regular shelf price.

"Phone Scams to Get Your Money"

1. Con artists use phone scams to get money from people.
2. **The Sweepstakes Pitch:** The caller says you have won a big prize, but you need to send some money first to pay for taxes or other fees. People send in the money, but never receive the big prize.

   The Grandparent Scam: Someone contacts an elderly person and pretends to be a grandchild in trouble. The grandparent sends money to help and then finds out that their grandchild never contacted them.

Writing

Model Paragraph

1. The writer is trying to explain how con artists cheat people out of money.
2. Topic sentence: There are several ways that con artists persuade people to give away their money.
3. Examples used to support the point of view.

Exercise A

1. Topic: sale items price
   Controlling idea: not always special
2. Topic: American swindler Victor Ponzi
   Controlling idea: one of the greatest swindlers
3. Topic: going to garage sales
   Controlling idea: enjoyed most
4. Topic: con artists take people's money
   Controlling idea: feel no remorse
5. Topic: key to not getting ripped off
   Controlling idea: being careful

Exercise B

a) 5
b) 2
c) 3
d) 3

e) 4
f) 2
g) 4
h) 3
i) 1
j) 3

Exercise C

Topic Sentence: The best place to find a great bargain is at a garage sale.

General Point 1 (Reason): People sell both new and used items cheap just to get rid of them.

Example for Point 1: Last year I purchased a new $50 marble cheese tray with pewter handles and cheese knives still in the box for $3.

Example for Point 1: I picked up several bestsellers for $1 each.

Commentary on Point 1: Getting great bargains like these makes going to garage sales worthwhile.

General Point 2 (Reason): Occasionally, people sell valuable items that they think are worthless.

Example for Point 2: I heard about one man who bought a painting for fifty bucks that turned out to be a painting by someone famous worth millions.

Example for Point 2: My aunt picked up a vase for fifty cents that she sold to a collector for $500.

Commentary on Point 2: If you are knowledgeable about art or antiques you may be able to scoop up a valuable find for next to nothing.

Concluding Sentence: Going to garage sales during the summer can be a lot of fun and who knows—you may even get the buy of a lifetime.

Exercise D

1. b, c
2. a, d
3. a, d

Exercise E

Possible answers:

1. If the sale priced item costs the same every week, the sale price is not a special price.
2. With the discounted coupons and pyramid scheme, Victor Ponzi swindled people out of a lot of money.
3. Who doesn't enjoy looking for treasures and getting a deal?

Exercise F

1. for instance
2. moreover
3. consequently
4. as a result
5. for example
6. first of all, second
7. also
8. furthermore

Academic Word List

Exercise A

1. transfer
2. contact
3. individual
4. purchase
5. register
6. specifically
7. item
8. target
9. strategies
10. assume

Exercise B

2. **còn** / tacts
3. in / di / **vĭd** / u /al
4. **ĭ** / tem
5. **pŭr** / chase
6. **rĕg** / is / ter
7. spe / **cĭf** / ic / al / ly
8. **străt** / e / gies
9. **tăr** / gets
10. **trăns** / fer

Exercise C

1. assume (v): assumption (n) assumed (adj)
2. contact (v): contact (n)
3. individual (n): individual (adj) individualize (v) individually (adv) individuality (n)
4. item (n): itemize (v)
5. purchase (v): purchase (n) purchasing (adj) purchaser (n)
6. register (v): registration (n)
7. specifically (adv): specific (adj) specification (n)
8. strategies (n): strategize (v) strategic (adj) strategically (adv) strategist (n)
9. targets (v): target (n)
10. transfer (n): transferable (adj) transferability (n) transfer (v)

Exercise E

1. individual
2. targeted
3. purchased
4. assumed
5. contacted
6. item
7. specifically
8. transfer
9. strategy
10. registered

Unit 6

Vocabulary

Exercise A
1. f
2. d
3. i
4. c
5. j
6. g
7. e
8. h
9. a
10. b

Exercise B
1. assaulted
2. broke into
3. are investigating
4. accused
5. convicted
6. stole
7. arrested
8. murder
9. booked her / the woman
10. is wanted

Exercise C

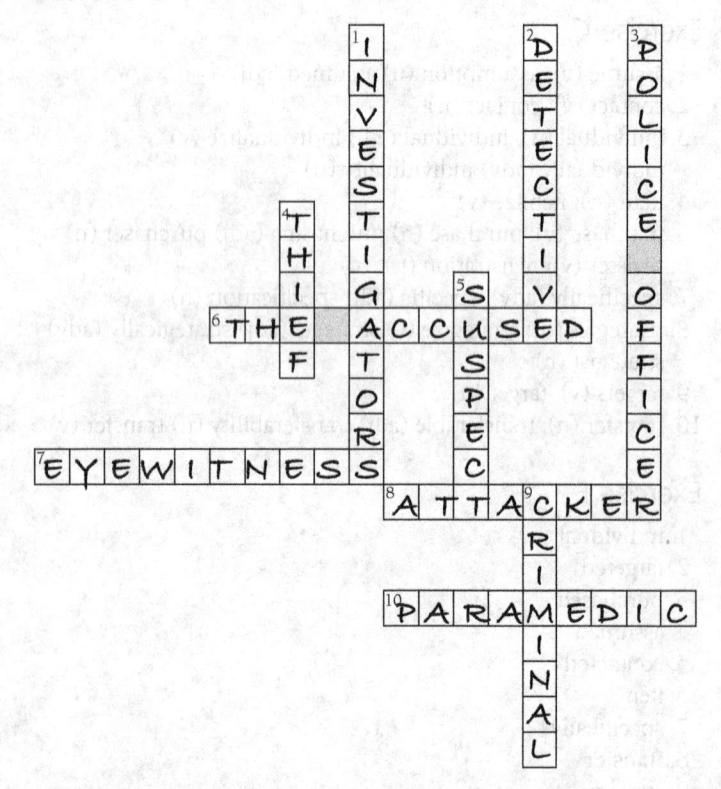

Crossword:
1. INVESTIGATOR
2. DETECTIVE
3. POLICE OFFICE
4. THIEF
5. SUSPECT
6. THE ACCUSED
7. EYEWITNESS
8. ATTACKER
9. CRIMINAL
10. PARAMEDIC

Exercise D
1. vandalism
2. firearms
3. arson
4. abduction
5. theft
6. fingerprints
7. forensic evidence
8. photographs
9. shoplifting
10. alibi
11. victim

Vocabulary Expansion

Exercise E
of: accuse, convict
for: arrest, be wanted, book someone, investigate
into: break
from: steal

Exercise F
1. arrested for
2. booked for
3. break into
4. accused of
5. is wanted for
6. investigating for
7. stole from
8. convicted of

Grammar Focus

Exercise A
1. The fingerprints are collected at the crime scene.
2. The murderer might be identified soon.
3. Evidence could be found at the scene.
4. Lots of pictures of the scene are taken.
5. The thief may be identified using trace evidence.
6. Blood splatters are used to determine what happened.
7. Insect evidence is collected to help establish time of death.
8. Millions of dollars were stolen from the armoured truck.

Exercise B
1. c
2. c
3. a
4. a
5. d
6. b
7. c
8. a

Exercise C
1. was robbed
2. was murdered
3. was found
4. were sent

5. was found by Heinrich
6. was delivered
7. were informed
8. were used by Heinrich
9. were questioned by the police
10. was identified
11. was arrested

Exercise D

1. A valuable coin collection was taken.
2. No change.
3. No change.
4. The entire room was dusted for fingerprints.
5. Three partial fingerprints and one good print were found.
6. The fingerprints were run through CODIS.
7. No change.
8. No change.

Grammar Edit

Late last night, an unknown intruder broke into the home of millionaire Jared Singh. Police say that the intruder broke in through a window at the back of the house that ~~will be left open~~ **had been left open** by mistake. Fingerprints ~~were find~~ **were found** on the windowsill and glass. Investigators used black powder to highlight the fingerprint patterns. Dozens of pictures ~~were be taken~~ **were taken** as evidence. A boot print ~~will also be found~~ **was also found** in one of the rooms. It indicates that the thief wears a size 11 shoe. A large quantity of cash and jewellery ~~was take~~ **was taken**. Singh reported that a diamond ring that had been in his family for over three generations was missing. Also stolen, was a priceless painting by Degas that had hung in his study. Local pawn shops and art dealers ~~have be notified~~ **have been notified** to be on the lookout for the stolen goods. The police think that the robber will try to sell the items quickly. Singh ~~will be questioned~~ **was questioned** by the police for several hours. They wanted to know why his security system was not on last night. Singh reported that the security system ~~had been turn~~ **had been turned** on before he went out for the evening. Now the police suspect that the thief must have been someone who was familiar with the home and knew how to disable the security alarm.

Guided Summary

	The Crime	**The Investigation Process**
The Crime Scene	1. An empty factory at the corner of Queen St. and Jones Ave. 2. A body with a visible head wound.	1. They gather important pieces of evidence including fingerprints, blood, and insect activity.
Fingerprints	3. Fingerprints from the victim's hand and others found at the crime scene.	2. They are collected using a live-scan machine and dusting. 3. They have different patterns of ridges. 4. Prints are run through a database called AFIS.
Blood File	4. Around the victim's head, on the floor 5. They take pictures and they use violet light beams.	5. They use a high-powered light. 6. They take photographs of the blood and samples. 7. They use the blood-spatter pictures to determine the angle the blood hit the surface. They collect samples from all the different areas. 8. They identify the DNA and run it through CODIS to try and determine a match.
Insect Evidence	6. Eggs and maggots from insects found on the body. 7. They can use the lifecycle of the insect to approximate the time of death.	9. They collect them and take them back to the lab. 10. They use the lifecycle of the insect to help establish time of death.

Writing

Model Paragraph

1. To explain the process of getting fingerprints
2. Collecting fingerprints
3. In chronological order of steps that must be completed
4. first, next, then, the next step, the final step
5. gently, quick, lightly

Exercise A

1. b
2. c
3. a
4. a
5. c
6. a

Exercise B

1. ~~You should~~ Lock all windows
2. ~~I think you should~~ Install motion sensitive lights around the outside of your house.
3. ~~You must~~ Put all ladders in the garage.
4. ~~I advise you to~~ Put bars on the basement windows.
5. ~~You are also advised to~~ Stop delivery of all papers and mail.

Exercise C

1. The digital scan is entered into the computer program.
2. Distinctive fingerprint patterns are identified.
3. The fingerprint patterns are compared against the database.
4. Matches with prints in the data system are identified.
5. The fingerprint information is used to identify suspects.
6. The fingerprint analysis can be used as evidence.

Exercise D

Order: b, h, f, g, a, c, e, d
1. next step
2. then
3. finally
4. once
5. the first
6. then
7. to begin

Academic Word List

Exercise A

1. a
2. b
3. c
4. b
5. c
6. b
7. a
8. c
9. b
10. c

Exercise B

2. ap / **próx** / i / mate / ly
3. **és** / ti / mate
4. **im** / age
5. **in** / dex
6. in / ves / ti / **gá** / tion
7. oc / **cúrred**
8. **pé** / ri / od
9. **pré** / vi / ous / ly
10. re / **móve**

Exercise C

1. analysis (n): analyze (v) analytical (adj)
2. approximately (adv): approximate (adj) approximation (n)
3. estimate (v): estimation (n) estimated (adj) estimate (n)
4. image (n): imagination (n) imagine (v) imaginative (adj)
5. index (n): index (v)
6. investigation (n): investigate (v) investigative (adj)
7. occur (v): occurrence (n)
8. period (n): periodically (adv) periodic (adj)
9. previously (adv): previous (adj)
10. remove (v): removal (n) removable (adj)

Exercise E

1. occurred
2. image
3. removed
4. evidence
5. approximately
6. investigation
7. period
8. analysis
9. previously
10. index

Unit 7
Vocabulary

Exercise A

1. corruption
2. unethical
3. illegally
4. consequences
5. behaviour
6. cheating
7. harm
8. accountable
9. guilty
10. fair

Exercise B

1. behaviour
2. corruption
3. consequences
4. legal
5. honest
6. ethical
7. guilty
8. fair
9. harmful
10. steal
11. accountable
12. lie
13. cheat

Exercise E

1. disorganized
2. disbelief
3. unfairly
4. unaccountable
5. illegal
6. impossible
7. irresponsible
8. immoral
9. dishonesty
10. disloyalty
11. unhealthy
12. unethical
13. inconsequential
14. illogical

Exercise D

1. impatient, imperfect, impersonal, impossible
2. disagree, disapprove, dissatisfaction, distrust
3. unafraid, unbelievable, uncertain, unusual
4. independent, inessential, informal, insecure
5. illegal, illiterate, illogical, illegitimate
6. irrational, irregular, irrelevant, irreplaceable

Grammar Focus

Exercise A
Possible answers:
a) If you lied to me, 4
b) If I lied on my job application, 6
c) If government officials didn't treat people fairly, 7
d) If the student were caught cheating on a test, 5
e) If I knew he had committed a crime and the police asked me about it, 3
f) If I already knew what to do, 2
g) If society didn't have laws to punish us when we behave badly, 9
h) If she had to choose between right and wrong, 8
i) If he broke the law, 10
j) If she took the money from his wallet without asking, 1

Exercise B

1. will treat / treat ... are
2. catches ... will take ... (will) give
3. published ... could sue
4. asked ... would fire
5. does not rent ...is breaking / did not rent ... has broken
6. has ... steals
7. hit ... left ... would look ... (would) arrest
8. set ... would go
9. beats ... is breaking
10. cheated ... would feel

Exercise C
Answers will vary.

Exercise D
Answers will vary.

Grammar Edit

1. will go down: Crime **would** go down if Canada had the death penalty.
2. Unnecessary comma: Fewer students would finish high school (**no comma**) if a high school education wasn't free.
3. did have not: If actions **didn't have** consequences, ethics wouldn't matter.
4. run: If businesses **ran** health care instead of the government, Canada would have better health care.
5. didn't be: Workers **wouldn't be** motivated to work well if companies didn't reward them with good pay.
6. Comma missing: If gay marriages weren't legal in Canada, people would be less tolerant of a gay lifestyle.
7. people still behave: If religion didn't exist, people **would still behave** ethically.
8. would stole: If someone in my family **stole** a car, I would lie to the police to protect them.
9. ban smoking: If the government **banned smoking** altogether, the cost of health care would go down.
10. If didn't treat laws people: **If laws didn't treat people** fairly, people would demonstrate.

11. Unnecessary comma: It wouldn't be fair (**no comma**) if some students were punished for plagiarizing while others were not.
12. if had to retire women: It wouldn't be fair **if women had to retire** earlier than men.

Reading

Joost Steffensen
1. Downloading music is ethical.
2. He thinks it isn't stealing because when you make a copy, the original still exists.
3. When you download music illegally, the artist doesn't make money.
4. People buy an artist's music as a result of increased advertising.
5. They offer products that are more expensive but less convenient than free copies.
6. They don't let people transfer music from one technology to another.
7. Computer games bought on a console can't be copied onto your PC.
8. It should get out of the distribution business and focus on rights management.
9. Users should keep downloading.

Goessl
1. Downloading music is unethical.
2. It's stealing.
3. People don't understand the ethical considerations of illegally downloading music.
4. Burning a copy of a CD for a friend is the same as taking songs off the Internet.
5. Musicians don't lose money when you copy a CD for a friend, but with file sharing millions of people can get copies for free. Therefore, the artist isn't paid.
6. No one wants to pay $20 for something they can download for free.
7. People think artists make too much money anyway.
8. Artists—because they own the music.
9. Because downloading music is quick and easy, there is little time to think about what you are doing.
10. Music piracy is morally wrong.

Writing

Model Paragraph
1. The writer is analyzing the causes of something.
2. Topic: cheating in higher education; Topic sentence: Excessive pressure to succeed, peer acceptance of cheating, and poor teaching all cause students to cheat in colleges and universities.
3. The writer makes three different points: pressure to succeed, peer acceptance of cheating, and poor teaching
4. The points are organized by order of importance.
5. The writer uses explanations (reasoning) in the analysis.

Exercise A
1. as a result of + C
2. because of + C
3. Consequently, + E
4. leads to + E
5. results in + E
6. result from + C
7. Therefore, + E
8. since + C
9. caused + E
10. so + E

Exercise B
Possible answers:
1. result in / lead to
2. causes
3. because of / as a result of
4. Consequently, / Therefore / As a result
5. leads to
6. so
7. results from
8. Since / Because

Exercise E
b) and c) will vary
1. C
2. E
3. E

Academic Word List

1. c
2. a
3. a
4. a
5. b
6. c
7. a
8. b
9. a
10. c

Exercise B
2. com / **mit**
3. com / **pu** / ter
4. con / **clu** / sion
5. con / **sum** / er
6. dis / **tri** / bute
7. **fi** / nal
8. **fo** / cus
9. **tape**
10. tech / **nique**

Exercise C
1. available (adj): availability (n)
2. commit (v): no other common form with this meaning,

3. compute (v): computer (n)
4. conclusion (n): conclude (v) conclusive (adj)
5. consumer (adj): consumer (n) consumption (n) consume (v)
6. distribute: (v) distribution (n) distributor (n)
7. final (adj): finally (adv)
8. focus (v): focus (n) focused (adj)
9. tape (n): tape (v)
10. technique (n): no other common form with this meaning

Exercise E
1. techniques
2. computer
3. distributed
4. available
5. taping

Exercise E
6. committing
7. conclusion
8. focuses
9. consumers
10. final

Unit 8

Vocabulary

Exercise A

Crossword:
1. CARING
3. MATURE
6. RESPECTFUL
7. HONEST
8. OBSESSIVE
10. STUBBORN
11. RESPONSIBLE
12. HUMOROUS
13. MANIPULATIVE

Down: CONTROLLING, JEALOUS, RURAL, OUTGOING, TRUSTWORTHY

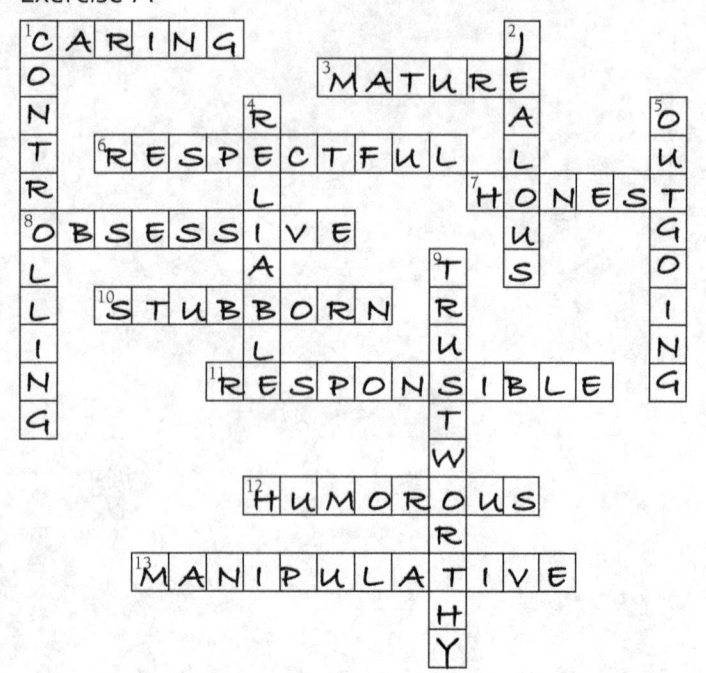

Exercise B

1. a
2. a
3. a
4. b
5. a
6. b
7. a
8. a
9. b
10. b
11. b
12. a
13. a
14. b

Exercise C

1. **dis**agreeable
2. **un**caring
3. **un**controllable
4. **un**ethical
5. **dis**honest
6. **im**mature
7. **im**moral
8. **un**pleasant
9. **im**polite
10. **un**predictable
11. **ir**rational
12. **dis**respectful
13. **ir**responsible
14. **dis**trustful
15. **un**trustworthy

Exercise D

1. disrespectful
2. disagreeable
3. irresponsible
4. uncaring
5. unpleasant
6. immature
7. unpredictable
8. irrational
9. untrustworthy
10. distrustful
11. immoral
12. uncontrollable
13. dishonest
14. impolite
15. unethical

Grammar Focus

Exercise A

1. that has
2. that doesn't allow
3. who / that thinks
4. that gives
5. who / that have lived / live
6. who / that marry
7. who / that are
8. who / that move
9. who / that have
10. that begin

Exercise B

1. He likes people who have a sense of humour.
2. Her parents want her to find a partner who is educated.
3. It is important to have a relationship that is healthy.
4. It is nice to have a family life that is peaceful.
5. Jennifer likes dates that are romantic.
6. Most people don't want a partner who is controlling.
7. Tim has a wife who is outgoing.
8. She married a man who is generous.
9. Some couples have marriages that were arranged.
10. They prefer movies that are exciting.

Exercise C

1. Nick has a girlfriend who is smart.
2. They went on a date that was boring.
3. He bought her a ring that was very expensive.
4. They went to a wedding that was fun.
5. Tina has a husband who is easygoing.
6. They celebrated their wedding in a restaurant that was beautifully decorated.
7. Do you think it's OK for a man to marry a woman who is twenty years younger than him?
8. He was married to a woman who was manipulative.

Exercise D
Possible answers:
1. Mary went on a **blind date that was organized** by one of her friends.
2. She is writing an **online-dating profile that will hopefully attract** suitable partners.
3. Are you going to call **the guy who responded** to your online-dating profile?
4. Is she still dating **the young man who moved** here six months ago?
5. Ben's girlfriend bought him **the computer game that just came on the market** last week.
6. Hatem thinks it is silly to make his children follow **dating rules that are old-fashioned / the same dating rules that he had to follow**.
7. Do you think it's OK for **young people who are still in high school** to date?
8. **The couple who had three children** were married longer (than the couple who had no children).

Exercise E
Answers will vary.

Grammar Edit
1. an evening that was fun or romantic (lines 3–4)
2. the roses that were in the bouquet (lines 6–7)
3. a woman who fell in love with her neighbour (lines 9–10)
4. a man who was a loser (line 13)
5. meat that is undercooked (lines 15–16)
6. vegetables that are overcooked (lines 17–18)
7. a restaurant that charges a lot of money (line 20)
8. the subway that they took (line 22)

Reading

Guided Summary
The paragraph will vary, but it should include the following information:
1. Anand Ram is a young man who grew up in the West, but whose parents and family are from India.
2. When he was growing up, he was confused by the differences between romantic love and marriage. His parents' Eastern traditions valued arranged marriages whereas Western traditions value romantic love. Romantic love seems to be the opposite of arranged marriage.
3. Anand learned about love from Western movies. He learned that love always wins. All problems are solved in romantic love like a puzzle.
4. Anand learned about marriage from his parents. He learned that romantic love is less important for marriage than joining two families. Western people value romantic love, but the divorce rate in the West is very high. In India, people have arranged marriages. The divorce rate is very low. Therefore, romantic love is not necessary for a marriage to last. When two families join together in marriage, they become interdependent. This means there is less chance for divorce.
5. He was young and he didn't understand his parent's point of view about arranged marriage. Now he doesn't question the tradition that has been in India for a long time.
6. The writer wants to mix the Eastern value of joining two families in marriage and the Western value of romantic love. He will not accept an arranged marriage. He will date before marriage to get to know his partner. He will disagree with his parents' about Indian dating and marriage traditions, but he will not lie to them about what he is doing. When he marries, he will keep some old traditions and start some new ones. He wants romantic love, but he also wants a marriage that will not end in divorce.

Writing

Model Paragraph
1. The writer's aim is to contrast.
2. Topic: traditional and modern marriages; Topic sentence: Traditional marriages like my great-grandmother's differ from modern marriages like my own in very important ways.
3. The writer first writes about traditional marriages and then writes about modern marriages.
4. similarities: both, similarities; differences: differ from, in contrast, on the one hand…on the other hand, but, differences
5. firstly, secondly, also, finally

Exercise B
Wording may vary, but concepts should reflect the following:
1. marriage
2. career
3. children
4. extended family
5. activities and interests
6. food
7. health
8. religion

Exercise C
1. Both … and
2. both … and, In contrast,
3. , but
4. are different from
5. Unlike …
6. Just as … also
7. On the one hand, / On the other hand,
8. Similarly,
9. likewise,
10. whereas

Exercise D
Answers will vary.

Exercise E

Answers will vary slightly.

1. The writer is comparing modern and traditional marriages.
2. Traditional marriages like my great-grandmother's differ from modern marriages like my own in very important ways.
3. The writer describes all of one, then the other.
4. differ, in contrast, on the other hand, but, also
5. Firstly, Finally, Also, Of course

Exercise G

Wording may vary slightly.

1. j) Arranged marriages differ from love marriages in that the families decide who is a suitable partner for the child.
2. a) Both speed dating and group dating are safe because you are not alone with the person.
3. i) Eastern traditions value the union of whole families whereas Western traditions value romantic love between two individuals.
4. e) In same-culture marriages, couples want their children to know their heritage. In intercultural marriages, couples also want their children to know their heritage.
5. d) In traditional marriages couples want the marriage to last. Likewise, in modern marriages couples also want the relationship to last.
6. f) Like Eastern parents, Western parents love their children deeply and want them to succeed.
7. h) Long-distance relationships can last a long time, but close-proximity relationships have a better chance to succeed.
8. k) Long-distance relationships are different from close-proximity relationships in that the partners can't express their feelings to each other physically.
9. c) Men are similar to women in that they want to find a suitable partner.
10. g) Unlike in face-to-face communication, in online communication it's difficult to show how you feel about someone.

Academic Word List

1. a
2. c
3. a
4. b
5. a
6. a
7. c
8. a
9. b
10. a

Exercise B

2. ap / **prò** / pri / ate
3. **àt** / ti / tude
4. **chàl** / lenge
5. con / **sùlt**
6. in / **vòlve**
7. men / **tàl** / i / ty
8. **mèth** / od
9. **nòr** / mal
10. **pàrt** / ner

Exercise C

1. approach (v): approach (n)
2. appropriate (adj): appropriateness (n) appropriately (adv)
3. attitude (n): no other common form with this meaning
4. challenge (v): challenge (n) challenger (n) challenging (adj)
5. consult (v): consultant (n) consultation (n) consulting (adj)
6. involve (v): involvement (n) involved (adj)
7. mentality (n): mental (adj) mentally (adv)
8. method (n): methodology (n) methodical (adj) methodically (adv)
9. normal (adj): normality (n) normally (adv)
10. partner (n): partnership (n) partner (v)

Exercise E

1. attitudes / mentality
2. appropriate
3. normal
4. methods
5. mentality / attitude
6. challenging
7. partners
8. approach
9. involve
10. consulted

Unit 9

Vocabulary

Exercise A

1. connect
2. associate
3. passionate
4. open
5. focus
6. aware
7. come
8. attention
9. improve
10. lead
11. reflect
12. think

Exercise B

1. leads (to)
2. aware (of)
3. connects (to)
4. associate (with)
5. think (about)
6. passionate (about)
7. (pay) attention (to)
8. came (up)
9. reflect (on)
10. focused (on)
11. improved (on)
12. open (to)

Grammar Focus

Exercise A

1. When did Shakespeare live?
2. Where did Leonard Cohen live as a child?
3. Why do children lose their creativity as they get older?
4. How can parents help their children to be creative?
5. What is the most innovative company today?
6. What classroom activities encourage creativity?
7. Why is innovation so important?
8. Who is the most famous poet in your home country?
9. How do you feel when you are creating something new?
10. What techniques do you use to generate new ideas?

Exercise B

Possible answers:

1. Who is/was Les Paul?
2. a) Why is he famous?
   b) What did he invent?
3. What was his job?
4. a) When did he play his first musical instrument?
   b) What was his first musical instrument?
5. a) When did he live? When was he born? When did he die?
   b) Where did he die?
   c) How did he die?
6. How many albums did he record during his lifetime?

Exercise D

Possible answers:

1. What kind of music do you like?
2. What is your favourite fantasy movie?
3. When are you most creative?
4. What kind of novels do you like to read?
5. Who is your favourite male actor?
6. Where is the best place for a fashion designer to work?
7. Why do children become less creative as they get older?
8. How do you stay creative?

Exercise E

Possible answers:

1. Why is this an interesting question?
2. When were TV shows like *Robotech* and *G-Force* popular?
3. Where did the film (*Akira*) do poorly?
4. What did classic anime films like *Laputa: Castle in the Sky* and *My Neighbor Totoro* combine?
5. Who is the most famous director of anime?
6. Why have there been a number of changes to the anime genre (in the last decade)?
7. How many episodes of *Pokémon* have aired on television?
8. Why is *Robotech* the most famous anime? / Why does the writer think *Robotech* is the most famous anime?

Grammar Edit

1. C
2. E: When will scientists find a cure for cancer?
3. E: Who are the most creative fashion designers in the world today?
4. E: Why is anime so popular?
5. E: Where are the best action films produced?
6. E: How can companies encourage innovation in their workers?
7. C
8. C
9. C
10. E: Where will you find the magnificent ceramics of Persepolis?

Reading

1. a) The writer aims to define creativity and explain the seven principles of creativity. b) The writer believes that if readers understand and develop the seven principles of creativity, they can become more creative.
2. Answers will vary but should include the following ideas: a) Creative people are very curious, b) Creative people test their ideas in practice, c) Creative people pay close attention to all their senses d) Creative people tolerate uncertainty, e) Creative people use both their analytical skills and their feelings and emotions when they think, f) Creative people develop and use both their minds and their bodies, g) Creative people make many different connections between things

Writing

Model Paragraph

1. The writer wants to show that sometimes creative ideas find him.
2. The story is about the writer musician and a woman. It happened on a train from Nova Scotia to Ontario a few years ago in October. The man met a beautiful woman who said something to him that made him think of a song.
3. The information is organized chronologically.
4. Transitional expressions include:

    a few years ago, at the time, at first, first, then, after that, after, before, at last

Exercise A

1a, 15b, 13c, 10d, 8e, 4f, 12g, 14h, 7i, 2j, 5k, 6l, 3m, 11n, 9o

Exercise B

Possible answers:

1. a) At first, b) After a while, a little while later
2. As soon as
3. a) At first, b) as
4. a) First, b) A little while later, c) Finally
5. As soon as
6. As

Exercise C

1. Last month
2. When
3. At first
4. after a while,
5. that night
6. After,
7. The next morning
8. that afternoon
9. now
10. A little while later
11. When
12. before
13. Now / Finally
14. Finally / now

Academic Word List

Exercise A

1. demonstrate
2. perspectives
3. creativity
4. environment
5. rely
6. principles
7. energy
8. affect
9. potential
10. research

Exercise B

2. cre / a / **tiv** / i / ty
3. **dé** / mon / strate
4. **én** / er / gy
5. en / **vir** / on / ment
6. per / **spéc** / tive
7. po / **tén** / tial
8. **prin** / ci / ple
9. **ré** / search
10. re / **lý**

Exercise C

1. affect (v): no other common form with this meaning
2. creativity (n): create (v), creative (adj), creatively (adv)
3. demonstrate (v): demonstration (n), demo (n), demonstrated (adj), demonstrative (adj), demonstratively (adv)
4. energy (n): energize (v), energetic (adj), energetically (adv)
5. environment (n): environmental (adj), environmentally (adv)
6. perspective (n): no other common form with this meaning
7. potential (n): potential (adj), potentially (adv)
8. principle (n): principled (adj)
9. research (n): researcher (n), research (v)
10. rely (v): reliance (n), reliable (adj), reliably (adv)

Exercise E
1. energy
2. creative
3. environment
4. affect
5. research
6. demonstrated
7. potential
8. rely
9. perspectives
10. principles

Unit 10

Vocabulary

Exercise A
a) Mountie
b) Inuit
c) francophone
d) First Nations
e) anglophone
f) multicultural
g) custom
h) image
i) lifestyle
j) stereotype
k) symbol
l) identity
m) prime minister
n) heritage

Exercise B
1. symbol
2. anglophone
3. Mountie
4. custom
5. francophone
6. prime minister
7. First Nations
8. Inuit
9. image
10. heritage
11. identity
12. multicultural
13. lifestyle
14. stereotype

Grammar Focus

Exercise A
1. singular, countable, unspecified
2. singular, countable, unspecified
3. singular, countable, unspecified
4. singular, countable, unspecified
5. singular, countable, specified
6. singular, uncountable, specified
7. plural, countable, specified
8. singular, uncountable, unspecified
9. plural, countable, unspecified
10. plural, countable, unspecified

Exercise B
1. The
2. the
3. Ø
4. a) a, b) Ø, c) Ø
5. a) Ø, b) Ø
6. Ø
7. a) Ø, b) Ø, c) Ø
8. the
9. a
10. a) A, b) a, c) the
11. the
12. The
13. the
14. Ø
15. Ø

Exercise C
1. a
2. a
3. a
4. the
5. a) the, b) the
6. a
7. a
8. the
9. a) the, b) the, c) a
10. Ø
11. the
12. the

Grammar Edit
1. a
2. a
3. the
4. the
5. Ø
6. the
7. the
8. a

Reading

Guided Response
1. Shayne Koyczan
2. Slam poem
3. Slam poetry is oral poetry written to be performed. Poetry slams are political events. The poems are passionate and address important social, economic, and political issues.
4. International audience.
5. Canada is more than the symbols and images people have about it
6. Answers will vary
7. Passion
8. Answers will vary
9. Answers will vary
10. When we say we are a strong and free country, it is not just words. It is true and our actions made it that way.

Writing

Model Paragraph
1. The writer's purpose is to explain what a beaver symbolizes.
2. The beaver
3. The dictionary defines beaver as "an animal with a wide flat tail and strong teeth," but for Canadians the beaver is much more than that.
4. a) provides historical information about the beaver: fur trade (1600–1800s), became symbol for companies (1600–1800s), postage stamp (1851), official emblem (1975), five-cent coin (current)

Exercise A
1. boat
2. (Canadian) money
3. (Canadian) sport
4. (Canadian) landscape
5. (Canadian) media
6. (Canadian) symbol
7. (Canadian) artist
8. religions
9. stereotype
10. (universal) human right

Exercise B
Wording and answers to c) may vary.
1. zipper
   a) Class: fastener
   b) Important feature(s): intertwining teeth, plastic or metal
   d) Dictionary definition: a thing that you use to fasten clothes, bags, etc. It consists of two rows of metal or plastic teeth that you can pull together to close something or pull apart to open it.
2. insulin
   a) Class: medicine
   b) Important feature(s): used to treat diabetes, regulates sugar in the blood
   d) Dictionary definition: a chemical substance that controls the amount of sugar in the blood
3. snowshoes
   a) Class: equipment
   b) Important feature(s): frame put on feet to help you walk through snow; oval-shaped
   d) Dictionary definition: a pair of flat frames that you attach to the bottom of your shoes so that you can walk on deep snow without sinking in
4. basketball
   a) Class: sport
   b) Important feature(s): played on a court, team of five, ball in hoop
   d) Dictionary definition: a game played by two teams of five players, using a large ball which players try to throw into a high net hanging from a ring
5. snowmobile
   a) Class: transportation machine
   b) Important feature(s): rubber track and skis to move over snow
   d) Dictionary definition: a vehicle that can move over snow and ice easily

Exercise C
1. f
2. a
3. e
4. d
5. c / a
6. f
7. b

Exercise D
Answers will vary.

Exercise E
Possible answers:
1. a) People often pour syrup on pancakes and waffles for breakfast.
   b) Maple syrup is a popular souvenir for visitors to Canada.
2. a) It was used by Aboriginal people as a way to transport people and supplies.
   b) A toboggan is different from a sled or sleigh because it does not have any skis on the bottom.
3. a) Black ice is not a thick visible layer of ice that you can easily see.
   b) Many drivers are unable to stop their car on black ice because they drive too fast.
4. a) People around the world recognize the bright red jacket, brown hat and brown leather boots of the Mountie uniform.
   b) The Mounties are a symbol of peace and order in Canadian culture.

Academic Word List

Exercise A
1. b
2. a
3. a
4. b
5. b
6. c
7. b
8. a
9. c
10. a

Exercise B
2. cùl / tures
3. de / **fine**
4. e / co / **nòm** / ic
5. **gòal**

6. **ìs** / sue
7. lo / **cá** / tion
8. **prò** / cess
9. **sùm**
10. sta / **tìs** / tics

Exercise C
1. chapter (n): no other common form with this meaning
2. culture (n): cultural (adj) culturally (adv)
3. define (v): definition (n)
4. economic (adj): economy (n) economically (adv) economical (adj)
5. goal (n): no other common form with this meaning
6. issue (n): no other common form with this meaning
7. location (n): locate (v)
8. process (n): process (v) processed (adj)
9. sum (n): sum up (v) summarize (v) summary (n)
10. statistics (n): statistical (adj) statistically (adv)

Exercise E
1. define
2. cultural
3. chapter
4. located
5. goal
6. statistics
7. economic
8. issues
9. sum
10. process

Appendix

A summary states the main idea of a text and the important information that supports the main idea. It does not include most details. When writing a summary, use your own words. You may not copy sentences from the original text, but you may use vocabulary from the text. The length of a summary is about 25 percent of the original text.

How to Write a Summary

Tips:
Before You Write

✔ **Preview** the text. Skim the title, subtitle, headings, first paragraph, first sentence of the body paragraphs, and the last paragraph. Get an overall idea of what this text is about.

✔ **Read** the text. **Underline** or highlight about 20 percent of the text as you read. Underline only what you think is important.

✔ Find the writer's **thesis statement** and say it aloud in your own words. A thesis is the main point the writer wants to make. It is usually somewhere at the beginning of the reading.

✔ Read through the text again and highlight only the key words or phrases that **remind you of the writer's main idea**. The highlighted words should equal about five percent of the article.

Write an informal **outline** of the text, using your highlighted words. Usually, but not always, an outline includes one main idea from each paragraph. Emphasize the points the author emphasizes.

Write the Summary

Write or type your summary from your outline. Do not look at the original text.

✔ State the **thesis** (main idea) of the text in your first sentence.

✔ Include only the important information that supports the main idea.

✔ Summarize the writer's **conclusion** (last paragraph) in one sentence.

After You Write

✔ Read through your summary and check that you have **used your own words** and have **not copied** sentences from the original text. Do not copy more than three words in a row from the original text.

✔ Read your summary **aloud**. Your **meaning should be clear** to someone who has not read the article.

✔ Read your summary **aloud a second time**. Look for grammar mistakes, especially in **verb tenses** and **subject-verb agreement**. Also look for mistakes in **spelling**.

The Paragraph

A paragraph is a group of sentences that develops only *one* central idea. The central idea is usually stated in a topic sentence. Every sentence in the paragraph must support this one central idea. Supporting sentences explain, describe, or develop the main idea. The conclusion of the paragraph usually summarizes or comments on the main idea. When the paragraph has only one central idea and all the supporting sentences develop only this one central idea, we say that the paragraph is *unified*. The length of a paragraph varies depending on how complex the paragraph is. It can be as few as three to five sentences or much longer. A common length for a paragraph in a short academic essay or test answer is between eight to twelve sentences. All the sentences in the paragraph must be complete grammatical sentences.

The Topic Sentence

The topic sentence is usually the first or second sentence in the paragraph, but it can also come in the middle or end of the paragraph. The topic sentence states the topic of the paragraph (what the paragraph is about) *and* the writer's perspective, attitude, or opinion about the topic. The attitude on the topic is also called the controlling idea because it controls the rest of the information in the paragraph. A topic sentence is not simply a statement of a fact. If the topic sentence is too general, it will be difficult to develop it sufficiently.

Supporting Sentences

All the supporting sentences in the paragraph develop the one central idea in the topic sentence. The support can include facts (and statistics), examples, explanations, details, or personal stories. Any sentences that do not support the central idea are considered *irrelevant* (unnecessary).

Conclusion

The last one or two sentences in the paragraph summarize or comment on the main idea. They bring the reader's attention back to the main idea in the topic sentence. Concluding sentences often repeat a few key words or a phrase from the topic sentence. A concluding sentence can also restate the topic sentence. This signals that the paragraph has come to an end.

Organization

Information in the paragraph is grouped into categories (information of the same kind). It is helpful to the reader if the writer uses words in the paragraph that explain how the ideas are ordered. We can use words such as *first* (*first of all*), *second* (*secondly*), *next*, and *finally* to show organization. It is common to organize a paragraph from the most important information to the least important information (or the reverse). We can signal this type of organization with phrases such as *the most important* (noun), *the primary* (noun), *the largest* (noun), etc. It is also common to order ideas from those that are most familiar to the reader to least familiar (or the reverse). Expressions such as *one* (noun), *another* (noun), *still another* (noun), and *the last / final* (noun) signal this type of organization.

Stating How Ideas Are Related

The relationship between sentences is stated directly with the use of words and phrases such as *therefore*, *however*, *even though*, *for example*, and *as a result*. When relationships are clearly stated for the reader, the paragraph is considered *coherent*.

Paragraph Outline

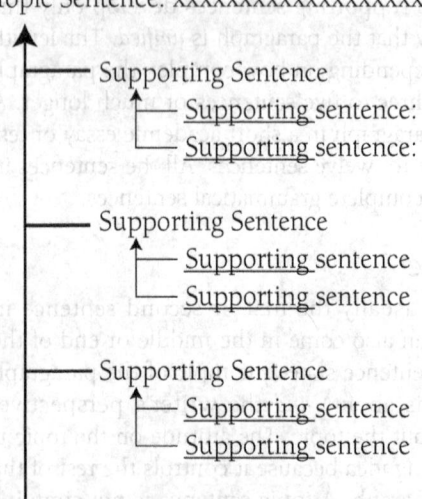

Topic Sentence: xxxxxxxxxxxxxxxxxxxxxxxxxxxxxxxxxxxxx:

— Supporting Sentence
  — Supporting sentence:
  — Supporting sentence:
— Supporting Sentence
  — Supporting sentence
  — Supporting sentence
— Supporting Sentence
  — Supporting sentence
  — Supporting sentence

Concluding sentence(s): xxxxxxxxxxxxxxxxxxxxxxxxxxxxxx

Words that Signal Comparison or Contrast

Part of Speech	Comparison	Contrast	Function
Coordinating conjunctions	and both … and	but yet	Coordinators join two words, phrases, or clauses of comparison or contrast. The joined units must be of the same grammatical kind: a noun to another noun, an adjective to another adjective, a phrase to another phrase, an independent clause to another independent clause.

Both Mayan and Egyptian pyramids are made out of stone.

Part of Speech	Comparison	Contrast	Function
Subordinating conjunctions	just as like	although even though though unlike while whereas	A subordinator begins a dependent clause of contrast or comparison and joins it to a dependent clause. If the dependent clause comes before the independent clause, place a comma after it; if the dependent clause follows the independent clause, don't use a comma.

Egyptian pyramids were tombs for pharaohs whereas Mayan temples were places of worship.

Unlike Egyptian pyramids that were built outside major cities, Mayan pyramids were built in busy city centres.

Part of Speech	Comparison	Contrast	Function
Conjunctive adverbs	also in the same way likewise in comparison similarly	however on the other hand in contrast conversely on the contrary	A conjunctive adverb of comparison or contrast signals a logical transition between sentences or paragraphs. Use a semicolon (;) or period before a conjunctive adverb and a comma after it. Conjunctive adverbs can also be placed at the end of a sentence. In this position they are preceded by a comma. They may also be placed in the middle of the sentence enclosed in commas.

The Egyptian pyramid in Giza is a world-famous monument. **Likewise**, the Mayan pyramid in Cholula is a world-famous monument.

The Great Pyramid of Giza was constructed following a single design over a period of 20 years. The Great Pyramid of Cholula, **on the other hand**, was constructed in four stages.

Note: *differs from* is a verb signalling contrast.

Photograph Credits

11 © iStockphoto.com/Jenny Leonard

22 © iStockphoto.com/David P. Lewis

24 © iStockphoto.com/Peter Spiro

25 © iStockphoto.com/Karen Locke

60 *The Scream*, by Edvard Munch 1893

86 © iStockphoto.com/Don Bayley

92 (clockwise, from top-left) © Photodisc, © Ingram, © Mint Photography, © iStockphoto.com/Ivan Ponomarev, © iStockphoto.com/creativeoneuk, © Photodisc

95 (a–f) *Oxford Picture Dictionary for the Canadian Content Areas*

96 (m, n) *Oxford Picture Dictionary for the Canadian Content Areas*